TOWARD FREEDOM books are moving narratives tracing the history of the black man's long struggle toward freedom in America. This three-volume set, written sympathetically from the black man's point of view, develops in dramatic detail important events that add new perspective for the reader and includes vignettes of famous blacks whose outstanding contributions moved their people toward freedom. The books will foster a sense of identity and pride within the black child and will help the white child to better recognize, understand, and appreciate the contributions of his fellow Americans.

Companion books dramatically tell the life stories of black men and women who have overcome great odds to achieve success in their chosen fields. Incident books spotlight the most exciting and significant episodes in black history and emphasize the black man's part in the growth of America.

Toward Freedom Series

THE LONG BONDAGE
1441-1815
by James McCague

GARRARD PUBLISHING COMPANY
CHAMPAIGN, ILLINOIS

Dr. Hollis Lynch, Professor of History and Director of the Institute of African Studies at Columbia University, is the consultant for the Toward Freedom books. He brings to this program experience as a teacher, author, and editor of West African and Afro-American subjects. A native of Trinidad, Dr. Lynch's lifelong involvement in black history includes an active membership in the Association for the Study of Negro Life and History and the African Studies Association.

Picture Credits:

Bettmann Archive: pp. 15, 23 (top), 30, 43 (top), 54
Culver Pictures: pp. 19, 93, 100
Metropolitan Museum of Art, Rogers Fund, 1942: p. 79
Metropolitan Museum of Art, Gift of Mrs. Russell Sage, 1910: p. 65
Picture Collection, New York Public Library: pp. 6, 22–23 (bottom), 25, 63, 88, 106, 124
Rare Book Division, New York Public Library: p. 43 (bottom)
Schomburg Collection, New York Public Library: p. 82 (both)

Copyright © 1972 by James McCague
All rights reserved. Manufactured in the U.S.A.
Standard Book Number: 8116–4800–1
Library of Congress Catalog Card Number: 74–151988

Contents

1. How It Began 7
2. The Slave Trade 14
3. Indentured Men and Slaves . . . 29
4. The Peculiar Institution 39
5. They Wanted Freedom 51
6. The War for Liberty 63
7. The Rights of Man 75
8. The Cotton Kingdom 87
9. Toussaint L'Ouverture 96
10. The Troubled Years 106
11. Into a New Century 116
    Index 126

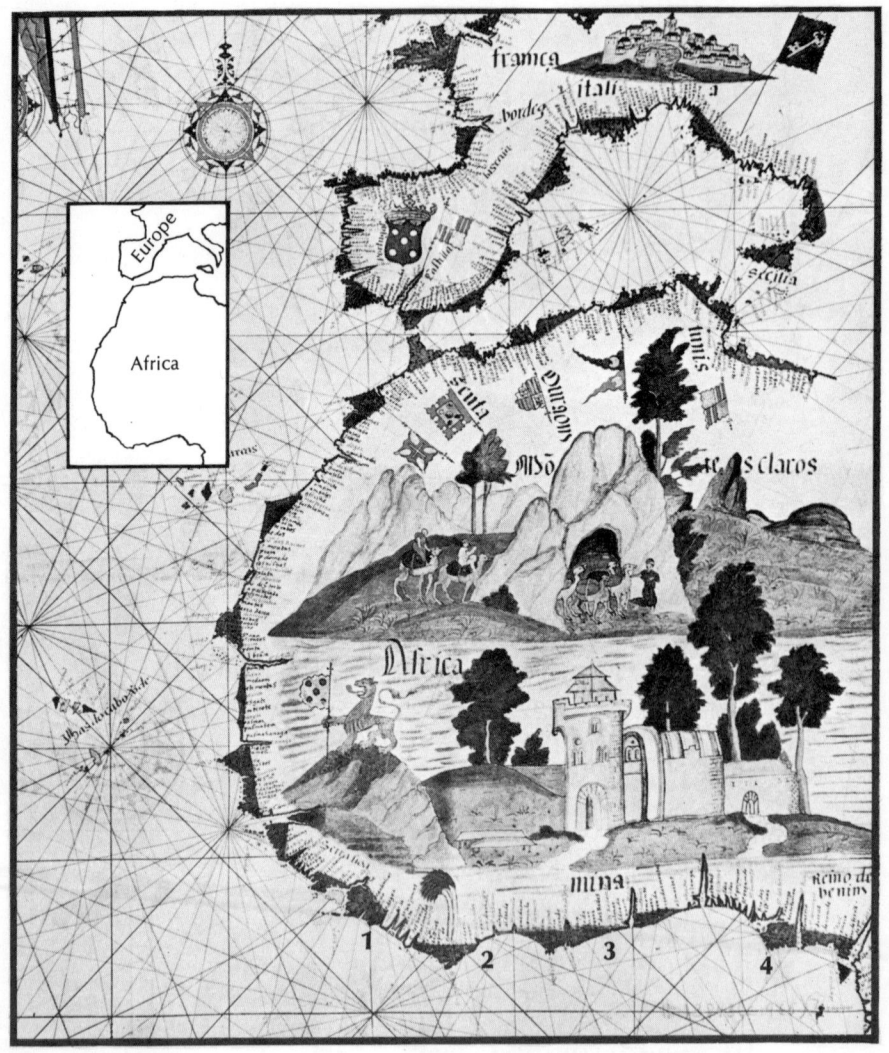

Soon after Gonçalves' voyage, Portuguese trading forts sprang up along the coast of West Africa, as shown on this sixteenth century map. Here the slave trade began and soon spread along hundreds of miles of coastline including the 1) Grain Coast, 2) Ivory Coast, 3) Gold Coast, and 4) Slave Coast.

1. How It Began

Captain Antão Gonçalves stood at the rail of his tiny ship and gazed eagerly out at the shore of the inlet where his crew had just dropped anchor. It was a day early in the long-ago year of 1441, on the western coast of Africa. Gonçalves, a young Portuguese nobleman, had been sent there by Prince Henry of Portugal on a seal-hunting expedition.

Seals were valued for their skins and for the oil which could be rendered from their fat carcasses. Young Gonçalves cared very little about such a dull, workaday mission. But he had been ordered to explore the region as well, and that was a task much more to his liking. As he wrote afterward, he "sought honor more than profit." He was about to find both, though probably not in quite the way he had hoped.

The world, as Europeans knew it in those days, seemed a much smaller and more mysterious place than it does today. The blue Atlantic Ocean, rolling mile after mile to the westward, was totally unknown. Men called it the "Sea of Darkness." Not even the bravest mariners dared to venture out into it very far. Few men, in fact, ever had sailed as far southward down the African coast as Gonçalves had. Africa itself was a vast land of mystery. No one knew what might be found there, though men in Europe had heard stories of a great kingdom filled with gold and treasure and ruled by a legendary king named Prester John.

With such thoughts buzzing about in his head, it was no wonder that Captain Gonçalves could hardly wait to begin his exploration. Leaving most of his crew to guard the ship and hunt seals, he took a few sailors and marched inland.

At first they found nothing but barren, sandy plains with no signs of human life. Presently, however, the sailors came upon a dark-skinned man, naked and armed with two javelins. Although he was outnumbered, he tried to defend himself as best he could. After one of the sailors had wounded him with a lance, however, the man was quickly taken prisoner. Soon afterward a dark-skinned woman was captured also.

Both the man and the woman spoke a strange language which the Portuguese could not understand. Well pleased with themselves, nevertheless, Gonçalves and his men returned to the ship with their prisoners.

The records of the voyage tell us nothing more about this unfortunate pair. They were taken back to Portugal together with several other Africans who were captured later. There they were sold into slavery.

One of the other prisoners, however, finally was able to make himself understood by his captors. Claiming that he was a powerful tribal chief named Adahu, he tried to buy his freedom with five or six other slaves. The Portuguese agreed. Adahu and two of his fellow black men were taken back to their homeland the following year. Though it is said that Adahu escaped without keeping his bargain, his companions did indeed ransom themselves by turning over ten other black prisoners to the Portuguese.

In this small way the slave trade on the west coast of Africa began.

As a reward for his exploit, Antão Gonçalves was made a knight and given a post as one of Prince Henry's aides. In the meantime more expeditions were sent out, with orders to sail farther down the African coast. Soon they saw that the nature of the land was changing. Farther north, it had been somewhat rocky and barren. The new regions, however, were green and fertile, with dense forests, great rivers, and a warm, tropical climate. Before long, the explorers came upon large tribes of black people living along the shore.

Many of these people were friendly, but others proved to be fierce and warlike. They sometimes fought the sailors who tried to go ashore. The white men usually had the advantage, though, with their heavy weapons and armor. More often than not, they defeated the black warriors and took prisoners, whom they carried off in their ships.

In the year 1444 one such expedition sailed into the harbor of Lagos, Portugal with 235 captive men, women, and children. Gomes Azurara, a historian of the time, has left us a vivid account of the occasion:

> On the following day, the eighth in the month of August, the crews put the boats in order at an early hour because of the heat, and led the captives ashore. It was truly a wonderful sight to see them all standing there, for some were fairly white . . . others were yellow . . . and some were black. . . . But who would have been so hard of heart as not to feel pity for them in their distress! Some lowered their tear-splashed faces, others bewailed themselves loudly and turned their eyes to the heavens, and still others . . . threw themselves to the ground. There were those who sang lamentations, and although we did not understand the words, the melodies told of their great sorrow. . . .

In order to divide the slaves into equal groups, Azurara added regretfully, "Fathers were parted from sons, husbands from wives, brothers from brothers." He went on to say, however, that most of the captives were treated with kindness by their new masters:

> They made no difference between them and their free servants, born in this country: but those whom they took when still young they caused to be instructed in the mechanical arts, and those they saw fitted for managing property they set free and married to women who were natives of the land. I never saw any put in irons like other captives, and scarcely any who did not turn Christian and were very gently treated.

Azurara, a gentle and pious man himself, no doubt told the truth as he saw it. Indeed, other accounts of those days show that the desire to spread Christianity among new peoples of the world was one very strong motive behind the early Portuguese explorations. Thus the saving of these black captives' souls, through baptism, was considered far more important than the fact that they were enslaved. Nor was slavery confined to black people alone. The Portuguese also made slaves of Jews and of the Moors who lived in North Africa and believed in the Muslim religion. Many of these, in fact, were very harshly treated because they refused to become Christians as the black slaves did.

Years passed, and great changes took place. Bold and daring seamen began to conquer the dreaded "Sea of Darkness." In 1492 Christopher Columbus sailed westward across the Atlantic. When he and his men returned safely, others were encouraged to follow. Gradually, over a span of years, Europeans came to realize that rich new lands lay there across the sea.

Spain, Portugal's powerful neighbor, was the first nation to found colonies in America, as the New World was called. Many of the first colonists brought black slaves with them, and many of the soldiers and seamen who helped to explore the vast, unknown regions of America were free black men.

It is believed, in fact, that a man named Pedro Alonso Niño, who served as a pilot on one of Columbus' ships during that first westward voyage, was black. When the Spaniard, Balboa, first discovered the Pacific Ocean in 1513, his party included thirty black soldiers. Other black men marched with Hernando Cortés, the conqueror of Mexico. One of them is said to have sown and harvested the first crop of wheat in the New World. Around 1530 still another black man, known as Estevanico, or Little Stephen, was killed by Indians while exploring what is now the southwestern part of the United States.

Plainly, therefore, black men arrived in America almost as soon as the earliest white men, and they played no small part in the exploration and settlement of the New World.

For a long time the Spaniards were able to keep most of the new lands for themselves. By the early 1600s, however, Englishmen, Frenchmen, and Dutchmen were also sailing westward to establish American colonies of their own. Some of them fought bloody wars with Spain and with each other in order to win and hold the new territories.

As their colonies grew and prospered, all these people needed more hands to do the hard work in their mines and on their farms and plantations. For a while they tried to enslave the native Indians from whom they had taken the land in the first place. But the Indians proved unsatisfactory. Unused to hard work and discipline, they soon sickened and died in captivity. So it was that more and more black men and women were brought to America.

These, however, came not in freedom, but in chains and bitter sorrow.

2. The Slave Trade

Bound together two by two with heavy wooden yokes fastened around their necks, a long line of black men and women plodded down a well-worn path through the dense forest. Most of the men were burdened with huge elephants' tusks. Others, and many of the women too, bore baskets or bales of food. Little boys and girls trudged along beside their parents, eyes wide in fear and wonder.

Everyone was footsore and weary. None of these people knew where they were going or what was to become of them. But they had little time or energy for thinking about that. Other black men, tall warriors armed with muskets and spears, drove them onward with shouts and cracking whips.

Only a few days earlier these unfortunates had been living happily in their village of thatched huts deep in the heart of West Africa. Then, early one morning, the village had been attacked by raiders from an enemy tribe. The huts had been burned. Most of the people, outnumbered and caught by surprise, had been killed or captured. Now the prisoners were on their way to the distant seacoast to be sold as slaves.

Such slave caravans, known as *coffles*, often had to march hundreds of long, weary miles to reach the sea. The way wound through dense, tangled forests, across broad, sun-baked plains, and over muddy rivers. The prisoners were driven without mercy. They were allowed only brief rest periods and scanty rations of grain or yams. Many of the weaker ones were unable to keep going. When they stumbled and fell, they were simply cut out of the coffle and left to die of hunger and exhaustion, or to be killed by wild animals.

Finally the nightmare journey ended. Ahead of them the slaves saw the ocean stretching away to the far horizon, with great, foaming waves rolling in to crash on a sandy beach. They saw a village of native

A caravan of slaves trudges sadly toward the coast.

huts clustered around the palm-leaf palace of the local chief, or perhaps the big wooden fort—called a *factory* —where a white trader lived.

Nearby, too, was a large pen, or *baracoon*, made of tall stakes sharpened at the tops and set upright in the ground. This was their destination.

Hundreds of such slave-trading stations were scattered along the Gulf of Guinea. This was the great middle section of Africa's west coast. From present-day Sierra Leone and Liberia—called the Grain Coast in earlier times—it ran east and south through the so-called Ivory, Gold, and Slave Coasts to the mouth of the Congo. Along this whole stretch of coastline, extending for several hundreds of miles, the slave trade prospered.

Portugal no longer controlled the trade. Drawn by the large profits to be made, other European nations soon had begun to take part in it too. By the latter years of the 1600s, Spain, Holland, England, France and Denmark all were sending ships to West Africa. The slave trade had become big business.

Most of the white traders in their factories were employed by large companies with headquarters in various European cities. But other shipowners were independent businessmen who ordered their captains to obtain slaves wherever and however they could. A great many of these independent slavers were Americans from the English colonies of Rhode Island and Massachusetts.

Unlike Antão Gonçalves and his companions of other days, the white men seldom tried to capture slaves themselves. Instead, they found it easier and much less dangerous to encourage powerful tribes along the coast to make war on their neighbors who lived inland. For centuries past, African tribes had warred among themselves, just as the nations of Europe did. Prisoners of war were frequently enslaved and made to work for their conquerors, or sold to new masters in other parts of Africa. Nevertheless, slavery never had been an important factor until the coming of the white man.

Some white men did not mind admitting as much. A well-known and very successful slaver captain named Theodore Canot put it very well when he wrote that ". . . three fourths of the slaves *sent abroad* from Africa are the fruit of native wars fomented by the avarice and temptation of our own race." Then he went on to explain:

> We stimulate the negro's passion by the introduction of wants and fancies never dreamed of by the simple native, while slavery was an institution of domestic need and comfort alone. But what was once a luxury has now ripened into an absolute necessity; so that MAN, in truth, has become *the coin of Africa, and the "legal tender" of a brutal trade.*

Another man, a doctor on a slave ship from Liverpool, England, kept a diary which tells how his ship lay at anchor and waited while a tribal war was fought:

> *Dec. 29th, 1724.* No Trade to-day tho' many Traders come on board; they informed us that the People are gone to War within Land and will bring prisoners enough in two or three Days. . . .
>
> *The 30th Day.* No Trade yet, but our Traders came on board To-day and informed us that the People had burn't four Towns of their Enemies, and indeed we have seen great Smoke all the Morning a good Way up the Country, so that To-morrow we expect Slaves. . . .

Sometimes, instead of waiting, a captain chose to cruise slowly along the coast while his crew watched for smoke signals on shore. The signals would show that slaves were to be had there. Then the anchor was dropped, and the captain went ashore in a small boat. If the trader was a black chief, there always had to be a certain amount of *palaver,* or talk, before getting down to business. As a rule, also, the chief would expect some presents, or *dash.*

Once a bargain had been struck, it mattered little to hardened traders that slave families were separated.

The records of one slaving voyage, for example, tell how a powerful chief, known as Randy King George, was given a large mirror, an armchair, a red coat and a blue coat trimmed with gold lace, and a number of other valuable gifts.

Once the palaver was over, the slaves were brought out for inspection. The captain had his ship's doctor examine each one very carefully. Mouths were forced open; bodies were poked and prodded; slaves were made to jump up and down, bend over, and run about. All this was necessary in order to make sure that they were healthy, strong, and active. Any man or woman who looked older than forty years or so was rejected at once. So were any who showed even the slightest symptoms of disease. These unlucky ones were either killed by their disappointed captors or else kept for a while in hopes that some other slaver might accept them.

The bargaining was always long and hard, for neither traders nor slaver captains had any scruples about cheating each other if they could. At last, however, a certain number of *pieces* were agreed on as the price of each slave selected. The value of a piece varied, but it usually was reckoned in terms of muskets, iron bars, rolls of cloth, or similar trade goods.

Some captains had the slaves branded with red-hot irons as soon as a trade was completed. This was done most commonly if the slaves were to be left ashore in the baracoons for any length of time. It prevented dishonest traders—and most of them *were* dishonest—from substituting old or sickly slaves for the healthy ones already paid for. But one slaver captain noted that in the branding, "care is taken that the women, as the tenderest, be not burnt too hard."

After some years rum came to be the best trade good of all, as natives on the slave coasts grew to crave it more and more. Thus we find one captain complaining in a letter to the owners of his ship that business was bad because he lacked rum to trade. "I have repented a hundred times ye laying in of dry goods," he wrote bitterly. Then he went on to name six other ships which were lying off the coast and competing with him for the available supply of slaves.

"All these is Rum ships," he added in disgust.

In such a case, a ship might have to linger on the slave coast for weeks, or even months, before filling out its cargo. The hot, damp climate was terribly unhealthy for white men. Sailors often sickened and died of malaria, yellow fever, and all manner of tropical diseases. Slaving was a miserably hard, cruel business in every way, and one would expect that none but the hardest and most degraded men could stand the life for very long. Yet there were many who came back voyage after voyage.

During the 1700s, most American ships engaged in the trade were quite small, with limited cargo space. A typical vessel would be fitted with a special slave deck in the hold, however. The space between decks, no more than five feet, provided scant headroom for an adult man or woman. Nevertheless, even that was considered much too generous, for every captain loaded his ship with as many slaves as he could possibly pack into her. To that end, rough wooden shelves, six or seven feet wide, usually were added between the decks on both sides, cutting the headroom to two feet or less.

In these cramped spaces the slaves were forced to lie on their sides, each jammed tightly against his neighbor's back. A flimsy partition, or bulkhead, separated men from women and children, and the men were chained together by wrists and ankles to discourage them from making a break for freedom. It was not uncommon for slaves to be stripped of every shred of clothing when they were brought aboard the ship, because even the scantiest rags might harbor vermin which, in turn, might carry disease.

Though the hatches overhead were covered only by wooden or iron gratings to provide ventilation, the

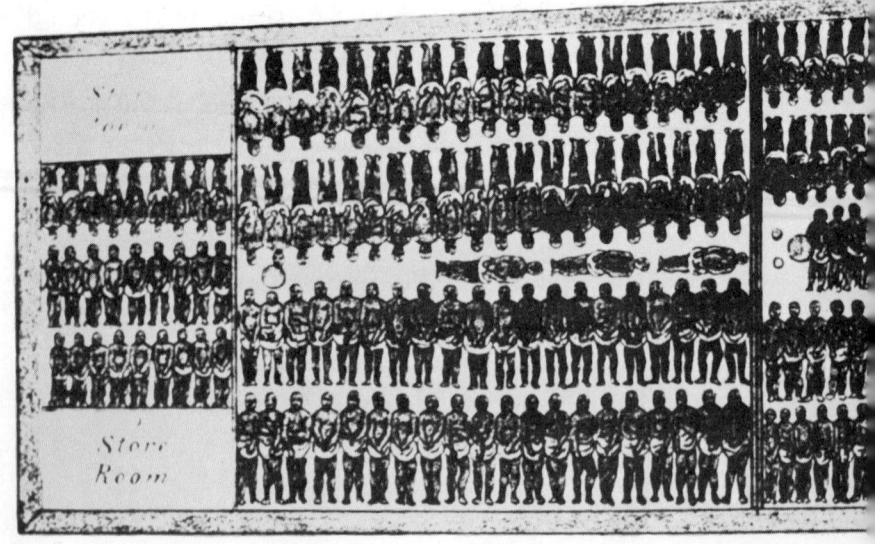

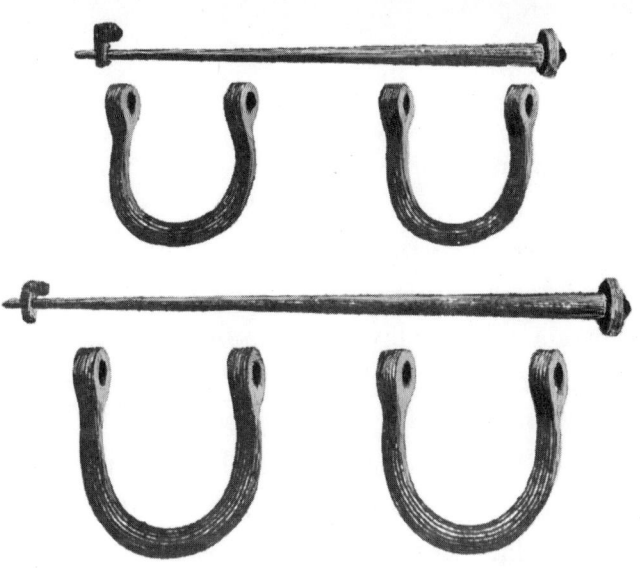

Not a square inch of space was wasted in this loading plan for a nineteenth century slave ship. Heavy iron shackles (above) were used to chain men together in the cruelly crowded hull.

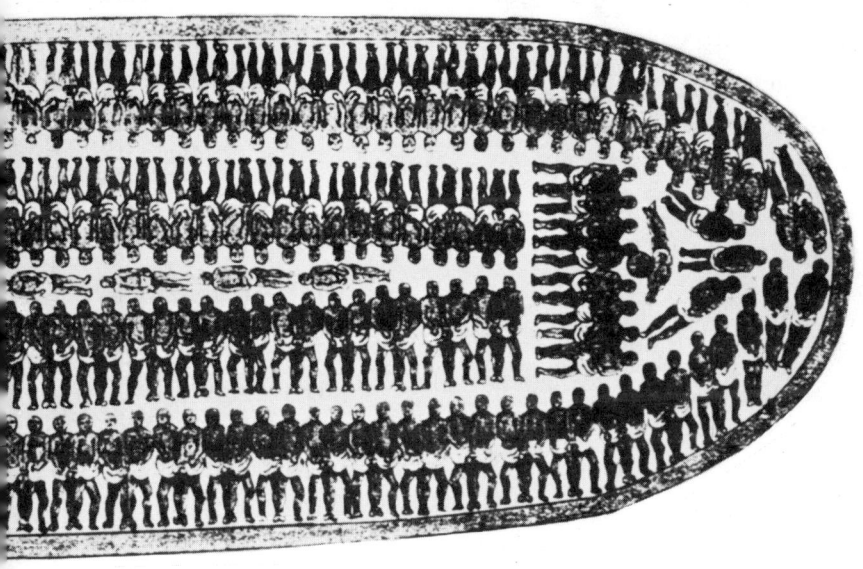

air in the crowded hold quickly grew foul and stinking. Fierce tropical heat added to the slaves' misery. So did seasickness, once the ship began to pitch and roll as it set sail across the ocean. Since the slaves had now become a valuable investment, however, the captain and crew usually did all they could to keep them alive and in good health.

At best, in overcrowded ships with only the crudest of sanitation facilities, it was little enough.

In fine weather all slaves were brought on deck twice a day for fresh air, exercise, and meals. Although they were guarded by sailors armed with muskets and cutlasses, the slaves were encouraged to move about as much as possible. Sometimes, in fact, they were compelled to dance and sing in order to raise their spirits, though it is hard to believe that such a spectacle could have been very merry. The food was coarse and unappetizing, but plentiful. Frequently it was a sort of stew called *slabber sauce,* made of beans, palm oil, and bits of salt meat or fish. This was cooked on the open deck in big iron pots and seasoned with lots of pepper, which was thought to help ward off fever.

During these times on deck, some of the sailors scrubbed the 'tween-decks thoroughly. The more docile slaves were often forced to help. Vinegar was used as a crude kind of disinfectant. Sometimes iron musket balls would be heated red-hot and dropped into buckets of vinegar, giving off fumes which were believed to purify the air.

A fast ship, running before favorable winds, might cross the Atlantic in about five or six weeks. But such a voyage was considered unusually lucky. Sometimes a ship ran into strong head winds or even storms. Then all the hatches had to be closed down tightly, perhaps for days on end, while the slaves below lay in pitch-darkness with barely enough air to breathe. At other times the wind might fail altogether, leaving the ship becalmed under a broiling sun till food spoiled and drinking water ran low. Under such conditions, frightful epidemics of cholera, smallpox, or other diseases were likely to break out, killing sailors and slaves alike.

The heavily armed crew of a slave ship prepares to stow its human "cargo" below for the night.

Even on a good passage, most captains expected a few slaves to die. The number of deaths varied widely, of course, depending on the circumstances. But most scholars believe that the mortality rate averaged about thirteen percent. In other words, one of every eight or nine slaves was dead before the voyage ended. The slavers accepted such losses as a normal hazard of the trade.

The slaves, however, were not always willing to accept their miserable fate. Some preferred death to slavery. Watching their chance while on deck, they might try to jump overboard and drown themselves. Many refused to eat and had to be fed by force. Occasionally, brave men managed to free themselves from their chains and rise in revolt. The history of the trade is filled with stories like this one, telling of an uprising aboard a ship from Rhode Island in the year 1765:

> Captain Esek Hopkins . . . had lost most of the crew and officers of his brig *Sally* through illness. When his ship had loaded its cargo on the African coast and set sail for the American continent, the Captain selected a few slaves who looked more alert than the rest and allowed them to move about the ship at will, in return for acting as crew members.

The slaves freed their fellows in irons and rose up against the captain and the white crew; the latter, however, were armed to the teeth, conscious of the danger that free slaves on board represented; they were especially careful because of their reduced number and the advantage that the more than 100 slaves on the ship held over them. Hopkins and his men met the attack with murderous fire, killing or forcing overboard eighty . . .

Once in a while, though rarely, rebellious slaves did succeed in overcoming a ship's crew. If the vessel was not too far from the African coast at the time, they could run her aground and make their escape. Still, the odds against them were always heavy.

The Middle Passage, as this westward voyage across the Atlantic was called, usually ended at Cuba, Jamaica, or some other island in the West Indies. The slaves were taken ashore and given a few days to rest and recover from the long weeks at sea. Then they were sold at auctions, either to the owners of the great sugar plantations on those islands, or to slave dealers who planned to resell them at a profit later.

The profits generally were very good. Though prices varied due to supply and demand, a prime slave

—an adult in good condition—usually could be obtained on the coast of Guinea for rum or other trade goods worth about fifty or sixty dollars. In the West Indies the same slave would bring anywhere from one hundred to two hundred dollars or more.

Most American slavers took at least part of this money in the form of barrels of molasses made from West Indian sugar cane. Then, sailing northward to New England, they sold the molasses at an additional profit. In New England the molasses was distilled into rum, and the rum was then carried to West Africa to be traded for more slaves. Thus the trade became a vicious triangle which went on with never an ending or a pause.

For more than 350 years this trade thrived. No one knows how many black men, women, and children became its victims. The best estimates, based on studies of the surviving records, indicate that a total of some 10,000,000 slaves were brought into the Americas, while another million and a half died on the way. Nevertheless, the trade meant wealth and prosperity to thousands of shipowners and other businessmen in Europe and America.

To the millions of slaves, it meant lifetimes of bondage and hard work in the strange New World.

3. Indentured Men and Slaves

"About the last August came in a Dutch man of warre that sold us twenty negars . . ."

Those words were written in the year 1619 by John Rolfe, one of the leaders of the English settlement at Jamestown, Virginia. They tell us all we know about the beginning of black slavery in North America, for the Virginia colony was the first permanent one on this continent.

Perhaps Rolfe wrote so briefly because he had no reason to think the event was important. From his point of view, no doubt, it was not. Virginia was a new colony, only twelve years old. It had no vast plantations like those in the West Indies, where slavery already was well established. Therefore the Virginia colonists had no need for large numbers of slave workers. They preferred at first to rely on indentured white servants, and English laws of the time made it easy to get all they needed.

The *indenture* system was actually much like a form of slavery. Englishmen and women convicted of

The arrival of twenty black indentured servants at the English colony of Jamestown, 1619

crimes often were indentured and banished to the colonies instead of being hanged or imprisoned. In other cases, poor people who wished to leave England agreed to sell themselves into bondage in return for their passage across the sea. Then the ship captain could, in turn, sell their indenture contracts to some colonist who was looking for servants.

An indentured person was bound to serve his master for a certain number of years, usually from two to eight, and seldom more than ten. During that whole time he received no pay except his food, shelter, and clothing. Generally he was worked hard. Sometimes he was harshly treated, and if he tried to run away, severely punished. When his time was up, however, he had to be set free and given *freedom dues* by his master. Such dues might consist of a small sum of money, or perhaps a tract of land and a few tools, to help him get started on his own.

Strange as it may seem to us today, the system worked reasonably well—well enough, at least, so that it remained in force in America, in one form or another, for some 200 years.

Apparently those first twenty black men of whom Rolfe wrote were sold as indentured servants, rather than as slaves. For many years afterward, in fact, black men and women brought into the colony and sold there were always referred to as "negro servants," never as slaves.

In a description of a certain Captain Samuel Matthews, a well-to-do landowner on the James River in 1648, for example, we find this:

> He hath a fine house and all things answerable to it; he sows yearly stores of hemp and flax, and causes it to be spun; he keeps weavers, and hath a tan-house, causes leather to be dressed, hath eight shoemakers employed in this trade, *hath forty negro servants*, brings them up to trades in his house . . .

Masters like Captain Matthews apparently treated their black servants neither better nor worse than their indentured white ones. Sometimes indenture contracts were written for them. Even when this was not done, their masters frequently set them free and provided freedom dues after several years, just as they did with the whites whose contracts had run out. Like the white servants, too, they were usually permitted to keep pigs, cattle, and other property of their own while still in bondage.

This was due in part to the kindness of individual masters, of course. But partly, also, it came about because no one really understood the black servants' legal status. English laws of the time did not recognize slavery. Hence no white man could be sure he had the right to make black men and women work for him all their lives. Further doubts arose because most of the black servants were Christians, or soon became Christians. Pious whites felt it was wrong for one Christian to enslave another.

For some years, then, Virginia seemed to offer a promising future to her black workers. Their lives were far from easy, it is true. But they were no harder than those of the poor white colonists. Indeed, white servants and black lived and worked together on equal terms. They mingled freely, sharing the same hardships and the same pleasures. Even marriage between the two races was not at all uncommon. White masters sometimes disapproved of such marriages, but during the early years, at least, seldom forbade them.

These conditions were not destined to last long, however. Factors over which the black man had no control were working against him. Matters gradually began to change for the worse.

The settlers found that Virginia's soil and climate were good for growing tobacco. Other crops they raised were barely enough for their own needs. Tobacco, though, could be shipped to England and sold there at a high price. Thus the colony had its first money crop, and landowners were soon clearing new fields and planting more and more of it. Before long this led to a need for larger gangs of field workers, for raising and curing the tobacco was a long, tedious job.

Indentured whites could be used, of course, and so they were for a while. But it was not very profitable. Sooner or later the white servants had to be released and paid their freedom dues. Unlike the white men, however, most black servants did not understand the indenture laws very well and had only a vague idea of their rights. White masters found it easy to hold them long after their indentures should have ended. Many began to do just that.

A case which was tried by the General Court of Virginia in 1640 showed where such a practice was all too likely to lead.

Three servants who had run away from their masters were caught and taken into court for trial. Two of them were white. The judges ruled that each man should have four years added to his term of indenture, a fairly common punishment in such cases. But the third runaway, a black servant by the name of John Punch, did not get off so lightly. He was sentenced to "serve his said master or his assigns for the time of his natural life."

So far as we know, the only difference between Punch and the two white servants was that he had not been formally indentured for a definite period of years. Apparently, therefore, the judges reasoned that the only sure way of lengthening his term was to extend it for life. Unfair though it seems by modern standards, there was nothing poor John Punch could do about it.

In this way, by custom at first, but soon by means of new laws as well, black men and women came to be bound *permanently* to the service of their masters.

They became slaves, in other words.

The Virginia General Assembly passed the first of the new laws in 1662. It declared that any child born to a black woman was to have the same status as its mother. This held true even in cases where the child's father was a free man, either white or black. Thus most black children born in Virginia after 1662 were doomed to slavery.

Not long after this, the Royal African Company was organized in London. Its business was bringing slaves from Africa to be sold in the American colonies, and England's King Charles II himself was its chief stockholder. In his eagerness to insure profits for the company, the king had still more laws passed to encourage slavery. Among the laws were some which limited the number of indentured white men who could be sent out of England. Thus, whether they liked it or not, Virginia plantation owners were forced to turn to the slave trade for the workers they needed.

Church leaders soon settled the old doubts about Christians making slaves of other Christians. If a person was not a Christian at the time his master bought him, they decided, it made no difference whether he was converted later; his status was unchanged. Within a few years another new law made this rule official by declaring that "conferring of baptism doth not alter the condition of the person as to his bondage or freedom."

Such laws did not mean that all black servants immediately became slaves. For a while it still was possible for many of them to work out their indentures and earn their freedom. Some—though a comparative few—not only did so but eventually acquired land and slaves of their own. At the same time, even as black slavery steadily gained ground, the practice called *manumission* grew right along with it. Manumission was simply the act by which a master freed a slave, whenever and however he chose to do so.

Sometimes a slave might be set free as a reward for exceptionally good service. More often, a master provided for his favorite black servants to be manumitted, or freed, after his death. Thus, as early as 1645, the will of one Virginia landowner included this paragraph:

> And for my old Negro woman (after my decease) to remain with her Dame till her Dame's decease, and then be free; and to receive two Cows with calf, two suits of

clothes, a good Bed and a Rug, a chest & a pot with four Barrels of Corn & a young breeding Sow; Likewise my Negro girl Temperance (after my decease) to be possessed of two Cows and to have their increase male and female; and she to remain with her Dame, to be brought up in the Fear of God, and to be taught to Read and to make her own clothes, and after her Dame's decease when she come to twenty years of age to be free. . . .

Obviously this man was a kind and generous master, deeply concerned for the welfare of his two faithful servants. But just as obviously, he felt it was his right to keep them in servitude or to set them free, whichever he chose. His kindness did not alter the fact that he thought of them, not merely as servants, but as lifelong slaves.

According to copies of old wills which still survive, many slaves were manumitted after the deaths of their masters. Apparently, however, Virginia's ruling white classes presently came to resent the growing number of free black men and women in the colony. Toward the end of the 1600s, the laws governing manumission began to be made much more strict.

By an act passed in 1691, for example, no master

was permitted to free his black slave unless he paid the cost of sending him out of the colony. Many masters were unwilling to do so; many others could not afford to. As for the slaves themselves, it was thought that they would lose their desire for freedom once they knew freedom meant they would be banished from old, familiar homes and surroundings. The wording of the act shows very clearly that it was designed to cut down the number of free black people in the colony because they were considered undesirable. The act read, in part:

> Great inconvenience may happen to this country by setting of negroes free, by their either entertaining negro slaves or receiving stolen goods or, being grown old, bringing a charge upon the country.

Such laws as this were not entirely successful. Manumission was never completely stamped out. By one means or another, black men would continue to earn their freedom and to live as free men throughout the long history of slavery in America. As the year 1700 approached, nevertheless, there was no longer any doubt about the status of most black men and women. They were slaves and would remain slaves.

4. The Peculiar Institution

During the years of Virginia's growth, various bands of English settlers arrived at other places in North America and founded colonies. Maryland was settled in 1634; the two Carolinas in 1663; Georgia, not until 1733. Farther north, Puritans fleeing from religious persecution at home had settled in Massachusetts in 1620, and other groups soon followed.

In less than 150 years, thirteen colonies had been established along the whole eastern seacoast. All were English, governed by English law. In all of them, as in Virginia, black servants brought by the early settlers soon led to the establishment of slavery.

Conditions in the northern colonies were quite different from those in the South, however. Neither the soil nor the cooler climate were suited to the raising of crops on large plantations. Most northern colonists either lived on small farms or depended on such pursuits as fishing, commerce, or the making of various goods for sale. Hence, there was no great need for large crews of field workers. Instead, white colonists who were prosperous enough to own slaves usually trained them as household servants or as helpers in a wide variety of trades.

This was a basic difference between North and South in our country. It had a deep and long-lasting effect on the course of slavery in the two regions.

In addition, the Quakers who first settled in Pennsylvania had strong religious feelings against slavery. So, to a somewhat lesser extent, did the Puritans of New England, despite the fact that many New England merchants and sea captains were engaged in the slave trade.

Thus, while a considerable number of these people did own slaves, they were generally inclined to treat them well and even to let them earn their freedom in time. This was not always the case, to be sure, but the practice became much more common in the North than in the South.

There, the black man's status went steadily from bad to worse.

Maryland was the first colony to discourage the mingling of black slaves and indentured whites by law. Her law, passed before 1690, was aimed specifically at marriages between the two races. Its opening words left no doubt about that. They read: "Forasmuch as divers free-born English women, forgetful of their free condition and to the disgrace of our nation, do intermarry with negro slaves . . ." Apparently, then, there still was very little prejudice against black people among the colony's poor white citizens. But the new law served notice that the ruling classes were not so tolerant. It penalized such mixed marriages by compelling the white wife to serve the slave's owner "during the life of her husband."

Moreover, any boys and girls born to the couple were to be slaves also, "as their fathers were." Virginia law already had made slaves of all children born to black slave mothers in that colony. Now in Maryland all mulattoes—people of mixed blood—were sentenced to lifelong slavery if *either* parent was a slave.

Maryland, like Virginia, was a tobacco-growing colony. But within a few years rice became the most important crop along the sultry, low-lying coasts of South Carolina, and later of Georgia. The cultivation of rice also required large gangs of field workers. The hard work and the unhealthy climate of the lowlands, however, constantly killed off great numbers of slaves. Since new ones were always needed, the slave trade grew more rapidly than ever. Presently, black men and women were being brought in by hundreds, and then by thousands.

The majority of them had come from the West Indies at first. But before long, slavers began to sail to the southern coast direct from Africa. Anchoring in such ports as Charleston, South Carolina, they advertised their slaves for sale in notices like this one, taken from a newspaper of 1784:

> A Cargo of very fine, stout Men and Women, in good order and fit for immediate service, just imported from the Windward Coast of Africa in the ship *Two Brothers*. Conditions are one half Cash or Produce, the other half payable the first of February next, giving Bond and Security if required.
>
> The Sale to be opened at 10 o'clock each Day, in Mr. Bourdeaux's Yard, at No. 48 on the Bay.

Buyers at sales like this one often judged the slaves not only by their physical condition, but also according to the African tribes to which they belonged. The Senegalese, for example, were said to be very intelligent and easily trained as skilled workers. Coromantees from the Gold Coast were strong and hardy, but known for their proud, independent spirits as well. Some white men would not buy them for fear they would be hard to manage.

Mandingoes, though good workers, were often too frail for the heaviest tasks. The Whydahs, Nagoes, and

This notice in a southern newspaper (right) offered for sale recently imported black men and women to be used as slave labor in the cultivation and drying of tobacco (below).

Juſt Imported in the ſhip GRANBY, JOSEPH BLEWER Maſter,

Seventy *Gold-Coaſt* SLAVES

of various ages, and both ſexes,
To be ſold on board ſaid ſhip at Mr. Plumſted's wharf, by
WILLING and *MORRIS*,
And a part of them are intended to be ſent in a few days to Dook Creek, there to be ſold, by Mr. Thomas Mudock for caſh or country produce.

Pawpaws of the Slave Coast usually brought top prices, being strong, willing workers. But slaves from the kingdom of Gaboon were considered almost worthless because they took to plantation life so poorly.

This kind of thinking was similar to the way in which modern farmers judge their various breeds of livestock. Indeed, most white people came to think of the slaves as more animal than human. In the minds of their owners they were simply possessions, or chattels, without any human feelings or rights of any kind. The law, in fact, backed this view by putting a slave in the same class as a piece of real estate. A distinguished Frenchman named Gustave de Beaumont who visited America was disgusted by this attitude.

It was easy, he wrote, for Americans to say that "a slave had no country, no society and no family." Then he added, expressing his scorn for such beliefs: "They made the slaves *things*; but by that they did not deprive them of intelligence and sentiments inherent in human nature."

Yet the treatment of slaves varied a great deal from place to place, even in the southern colonies. Nearly everywhere there were laws setting up rules which masters were expected to follow. They were required to supply their slaves with certain amounts of food and clothing, for example, though amounts often were barely sufficient for a slave's needs. It was generally illegal to work slaves on Sundays. On weekdays they could be worked no more than fifteen hours in summer and fourteen in winter.

In the early years, in many places, slaves were allowed to receive some education. Occasionally they even went to school with the master's own children. Many of the slaves brought in from the West Indies were able to speak Spanish, French, or other languages in addition to English. Any master lucky enough to own such a slave was quite likely to employ him as a teacher.

As time passed and slavery became more firmly rooted in the colonies, however, this situation changed. Masters came to realize that an educated slave was much more likely to become discontented with his lot than one who was kept in ignorance. As a result, laws were passed forbidding anyone to teach a slave to read or write. The usual penalty was a fine and up to six months in prison. In many localities—including some of the northern colonies—the ban on education was extended even to free black men and women.

Though practically all American slaves were Christians, marriage was not considered to be a slave's right. Indeed, since he was forbidden to enter into any kind of contract, a slave could not legally be married at all. Slave owners usually did, however, allow their black men and women to live together in what passed for marriage. In some cases the master might even "marry" such couples, in a ceremony performed by himself or —rarely—by a white preacher. But the relationship never was binding. Slave families could be, and frequently were, broken up—men and women and their children being sold to different owners—whenever their masters found it profitable to do so.

A slave had no property rights of any kind. He could own nothing unless his master allowed him to. He could not leave the master's plantation at any time without written permission. He was forbidden to drink strong liquor, to have weapons in his possession, or to keep horses, cattle, or pigs. He was never allowed to raise a hand against any white person whatsoever, even in self-defense. And the punishment for a slave who broke these rules was severe indeed.

Runaways, when caught, were flogged with as many as thirty-nine lashes. If they persisted in trying to escape, they were branded on the cheek with the letter "R," or had one ear cut off. This, of course, marked the slave for life as a troublemaker who was not to be trusted. If he still persisted after that, he might be hanged. A slave found guilty of stealing was whipped for the first offense, had an ear cut off for the second, had his nose slit for the third, and was put to death for the fourth.

Perhaps worst of all, the slave accused of any crime had little or no chance for a fair trial. He was never tried by a regular court. Instead, he was taken before a special one which generally consisted of two justices of the peace and two local property owners—all, of course, white. He seldom had a lawyer unless his master was willing to hire one for him. Moreover, no slave ever was permitted to appear as a witness against a white man who was on trial. This made it next to impossible for a cruel master or overseer to be penalized for abusing his slaves.

On his own property, in fact, a master had the right to punish a slave in any way he chose, and for any reason. A Virginia law of 1667 even went as far as to declare that the death of a slave because of harsh punishment could not be considered murder, "since it can not be presumed that . . . malice should induce any man to destroy his own estate."

In other words, the slave's status as a valuable piece of property was virtually his only protection against mistreatment. Simply because they *were* valuable, most slaves who lived by the rules were treated with reasonable kindness.

By its very nature, of course, the plantation way of life bound the great masses of southern slaves to toil at common labor in the fields, with no hope of bettering themselves. Everywhere, nevertheless—in the South as well as in the North—some slaves were trained for other occupations. They frequently worked as barbers, tailors, cooks, waiters, carpenters, sailors. Almost any job open to white workingmen, in fact, was often done by black men too. Some slave women were taught to weave and spin and sew, to serve as nurses, to dress their mistresses' hair, and to do many other things requiring skill and knowledge.

A smart and hardworking slave on a large plantation might rise to be an overseer in charge of other slaves. On farms and small plantations, masters and slaves sometimes worked side by side in the fields. In sparsely settled frontier regions far from towns and cities, it was not unusual for them to share their meals at the same table.

Now and then a master might allow an exceptionally skilled slave to have some free time during which he could work for other white men. Legally, any money earned in this way belonged to the slave's owner. But it was not unknown for a kindhearted master to let the slave keep all or part of it. If the slave was thrifty —as well as very lucky—he might eventually save enough to buy his freedom. Such cases were rare, although a few slaves did manage to achieve freedom by this means.

None of these privileges were true legal rights, however. The slave's master could always grant them or take them away, as he chose. And not even a free black man had any hope of being treated as the white man's equal—far from it! Though he was allowed to own property and engage in business, he had few other rights. Most of his activities were regulated by strict and unequal laws which kept him on a social level far below that of his white neighbors. At best, his actual status was only one small step removed from slavery.

It was true that some white masters were aware of the system's evils. As early as 1736 Colonel William Byrd, a prominent Virginia landowner, became convinced that slavery was a bad thing for the whites themselves. As he put it:

> They [the slaves] blow up the pride and ruin the Industry of our White people, who, seeing a rank of poor Creatures below them, detest work for fear it should make them look like slaves.

Colonel Byrd was quite right, and as time passed, others came to agree with him. In the South also, as in the North, there were white men who believed slavery was wrong for moral reasons. Some were bold enough to speak out against it, risking the hatred and contempt of other white men. They called it *The Peculiar Institution*, and declared that it was against all the laws of humanity.

Even the Virginia House of Burgesses, made up of leading citizens in the colony, passed a resolution in

1772 which described the slave trade as "that inhuman and impolite commerce." Nevertheless, the gentlemen refused to condemn slavery itself.

It was indeed a peculiar institution.

The simple truth was that slavery had gained too strong a foothold to be stopped. All slave owners felt sure that the colonies' prosperity depended on slave labor. In the South, where there was comparatively little commerce or industry, this certainly appeared to be true. In addition, there was a common belief among white people everywhere that black people were nothing but ignorant savages who were better off as slaves. This seemed reason enough for slavery and for the harsh laws designed to keep the slaves cowed and fearful and obedient.

People in the South had another reason, perhaps stronger than any. It was their own fear.

Slaves had poured in so rapidly, shipload after shipload of them, that before many years had passed, they outnumbered the whites in several southern colonies. Most were sturdy and work-hardened. Some, like the Coromantees, had been proud, fierce warriors in their African homeland. Given any opportunity at all they might easily rise up in rebellion, and their white masters realized it very well.

Soon, here and there, black men began to realize it too.

5. They Wanted Freedom

The first known case of black men trying to rebel and win their liberty occurred in Virginia in 1663. Apparently a small group of them banded together with some indentured white servants in a plot to overthrow their masters and escape. The scanty records of those early times fail to tell us how they hoped to do this or where they planned to go afterward.

In any event, the plot came to nothing. One of the white servants, known only as Berkenhead, turned traitor and told his master about it.

The old records say nothing about the punishment dealt to the rebels. Berkenhead, though, was rewarded very generously for his treachery. He was set free at once and given 5,000 pounds of tobacco, which was worth a large sum of money. The Virginia General Assembly also decreed that "the 13th of September be annually kept holy, being the day those villains intended to put the plot in execution."

Slavery still was far from common in Virginia at the time. Even the black servants were few, compared with the number of white settlers. Yet the General Assembly's action showed that the danger of an uprising by black men already was taken very seriously.

Perhaps it was no wonder. The colony still was small and weak and struggling for its existence. Hostile Indian tribes still lived in the forests near many of the settlements. Pirates or warships from unfriendly nations were likely to attack from the sea at any time. Thus the colonists could not afford to overlook any possibility of danger from within. This was true everywhere in America during the colonial era, and it may help us to understand the great fear of slave revolts.

Several other plots were discovered from time to time during the years that followed. Some were in Virginia, some in other colonies. All were quickly suppressed. There are indications, in fact, that many of these disturbances were not actually plots at all, but merely cases in which nervous masters *suspected* that their slaves might be up to some mischief. Frequently there was very little evidence to prove it. The so-called ringleaders seldom were put to death in such cases. More often they were flogged or sent out of the colonies to be sold in the West Indies.

Curiously enough, the first real slave rebellion broke out in New York City. On a dark night in 1712 a band of Coromantees and Pawpaws armed themselves with guns, knives, and hatchets and set out to revenge themselves on the people who had enslaved them. One claimed to be a sorcerer. He assured the rest that he had worked a magic spell so that they could not fail. All of them were proud, desperate men, and they meant business.

First the slaves set fire to a house. Hiding in the shadows nearby, they waited while a crowd gathered to fight the fire. Then they rushed out in a furious surprise attack. Nine white men were killed before soldiers hurried from a fort some distance away and stopped the fighting.

Six of the rebels killed themselves rather than surrender. The rest fled to the wilderness outside the city. But they were soon rounded up, tried, and sentenced to death. The sentences were carried out with terrible cruelty. One of the leaders was bound to a large wagon wheel laid flat on the ground. Then his bones were slowly broken with a sledge hammer, one by one, until he died. Several others were burned at the stake. Still others were hanged.

The laws for everyone were a great deal more severe in 1712 than our laws are today. White men and women found guilty of crimes were usually punished with great cruelty too. Even in those days, however, breaking on the wheel and burning at the stake were ancient methods of execution, inflicted only rarely and reserved for the very worst criminals. The people of

New York obviously looked upon rebellion by slaves with special horror.

That may or may not have been due to the fact that New York had more slaves than most other northern colonies.

Some years later another so-called slave plot threw the city into a panic. This time, however, it amounted to nothing more than a series of mysterious robberies and fires. Two white men and two white women, accused of plotting with rebellious slaves, were found guilty and hanged. Twenty-nine slaves were either hanged or burned at the stake, while many others were sent out of the colony and sold. The most tragic thing about the whole affair was that many of the vic-

When New York was New Amsterdam, the sale of slaves was already a thriving business in the new colony.

tims were convicted because of a story told by one white servant girl. Afterward, when it was much too late, the judges decided that she probably had lied.

In spite of white people's fears, most slaves who yearned for freedom preferred running away to trying to revolt. No one knows how many did run away, or how many actually succeeded in making their way to freedom. Certainly there were a great many, for we still can read scores of advertisements for runaway slaves in old newspapers of the time. Here is a typical one from a Virginia paper:

> RUN AWAY from the Subscriber in the Night of the 12th Inst., a Sailor Negro Slave named POMPEY, about 5 feet 5 inches high, and is Robust; he was lately bought of Mr. Perras, Merchant, in this Town; had on when he went away a brown Jacket and Breeches. Whoever brings him to the Subscriber shall have EIGHT DOLLARS Reward and Reasonable charges. Any Person harboring him will be prosecuted according to the utmost Rigour of the Law . . .

We have no way of knowing what finally happened to Pompey. Possibly, being a sailor, he was able to join the crew of some ship bound for a foreign land. But the odds were against most runaways, for they were hunted down relentlessly. Sometimes their masters trailed them with packs of fierce dogs. There were white men, in fact, who made their livings by chasing and capturing runaway slaves.

On the other hand, many of the runaways were described as being very intelligent. One advertisement mentioned that "as I expect he has a sum of money with him, probably he may get someone to forge a pass for him, and pass as a free man." It was not at all unusual for a runaway to have some money which he had earned or taken from his master, and of course, it gave him a much better chance of making his escape. Many, undoubtedly, were successful in making their way to some distant colony, where they were able to live as free men and women.

In the southernmost regions of South Carolina, a runaway slave's best hope was the Spanish colony of Florida. Throughout most of the 1700s, England and Spain were either at war or close to war. Therefore the governor of Florida was glad to welcome black fugitives, and Spanish law was in their favor.

The Spaniards, of course, were slave owners themselves. They sometimes treated their slaves with extreme cruelty—more so, in some cases, than the English did. In many ways, nevertheless, the Spanish slave code was quite lenient. Spain was a Catholic country, and the Catholic church insisted that all slaves be baptized before they were brought into any Spanish colony. As a result, the slaves always had certain rights as human beings which were denied them by the English.

One right was marriage by a priest. Furthermore, husbands and wives and their children never could be torn apart and sold to different owners. A slave could earn money and own property, not at the whim of his master, but by law. Most encouraging of all, he had a reasonably good chance of being set free someday. By custom, this often occurred when a master celebrated his own wedding or the births of his children. It was customary, too, for well-to-do landowners to free some of their slaves on every Catholic feast day.

Still another advantage lay in the fact that Spanish law always treated a runaway slave as a free man unless his master could prove him to be a slave. This was much better than the English law, which held that every black man was a slave unless he could show papers proving he was free.

Partly because of such laws, and partly as a means of defense against England, the Spanish authorities established a small settlement of free black men and women near St. Augustine, Florida, in 1726. The Spaniards gave it the long name of Garcia Real de

Santa Teresa de Mosa. Englishmen called it Fort Mosa, or simply Negro Fort. Each black family was given a plot of land, a few necessary tools, and some furniture by the Spanish government. Grateful for their opportunity, these black people worked hard, and Fort Mosa grew and thrived.

More fugitive slaves gathered there. A wall of stout logs was built around the town. A force of black soldiers was organized. Spanish officials trained them and supplied them with muskets and four small cannon, but they elected their own black officers to lead them.

Slaves in South Carolina began to pass the story of Fort Mosa secretly, by word of mouth, from plantation to plantation. The place became known far and wide as a haven for runaways. The English plantation owners fumed and worried. But they could do nothing, for England and Spain happened to be at peace during this period.

Nevertheless, they had good reason to be worried. Eleven years after the founding of Fort Mosa, South Carolina suffered its most serious slave revolt.

The rebels struck quickly and hard on a quiet Sunday morning while their masters were in church. Raiding a store in the small town of Stono, near Charleston, they seized some guns and ammunition and started for the Florida border. Old accounts of the incident tell us that they marched in good order with flags flying and drums beating, like an army. Along the way they burned several houses and farm buildings, killed a number of white people, and set still more slaves free. Only one of the white men they met was spared. He was an innkeeper whose slaves said that he had always been good to them.

It seemed for a while that the rebels might reach Florida, and freedom. Then, on the verge of success, they were betrayed by their own folly.

One of the houses they destroyed had contained a barrel of rum which they seized and carried off. Presently they stopped to rest and to sample the rum. As they celebrated their escape by dancing and singing, they were overtaken by a band of armed white men who had heard of the uprising and set out in pursuit.

The rebels' first hint of danger was a sudden volley of musket shots. Many were cut down at once. A few rallied and fought bravely till they too died. The rest scattered and fled. But every one was hunted down and shot. In all, twenty whites and more than forty black men and women were killed before it ended.

Still, there were other slaves who wanted freedom so badly that they were not discouraged. Less than a year later another band of runaways set out on a similar flight to Florida. This one was 150-strong. Without food or weapons, however, they too were speedily overtaken by white men. At least fifty were captured and hanged.

These were the biggest slave rebellions during this period of the mid-1700s, but they were not the only ones. Sometimes small parties of escaped slaves found their way into the dense forests and rugged mountains on the western frontiers of the colonies. Many joined the Indians who lived there. Others contrived to live for a while as outlaws. They ventured out of their hiding places from time to time, raiding lonely white plantations for the food and other supplies they needed. But none of them lasted very long. Sooner or later, all were found and destroyed by white soldiers sent to hunt them down.

Fort Mosa remained a free black settlement until 1763, when Spain was forced to give up Florida to the English after being defeated in a war. Fortunately, however, the Spaniards kept faith with their black settlers. They were all taken to Cuba to live in freedom.

In most of England's American colonies, the slave revolts led only to harsh slave codes becoming harsher still. Free black people were made to suffer too. Always looked down on as outcasts by their white neighbors, they came to be despised more than ever because the whites often suspected them of sympathizing with the slaves. At any time their homes might be raided and searched without warning if they were thought to be hiding runaways. Sometimes they were forbidden to hold church services or other meetings lest they use such gatherings to plot trouble.

When trouble did occur, almost anywhere, the free blacks were likely to be the first ones blamed. If found guilty of breaking even the most trivial laws, they could be—and often were—sold into slavery.

For several years, nevertheless, it seemed that the rebellions and rumors of rebellion might have at least one good effect. More fearful than ever of the growing numbers of slaves, many colonies began to pass laws to limit the slave trade. In some it happened quite early. Heavy import duties were levied on all slaves brought in from outside the colonies, or even from one colony to another. The new colony of Georgia, founded at Savannah in 1733, at first banned slavery altogether. One reason was a sincere belief by the founders that it was wrong. But another was explained in the colony's original charter:

> Experience has shown that the manner of settling Colonies and Plantations with Black Slaves and Negroes hath obstructed the increase of English and Christian inhabitants therein, who alone in case of War can be relied on for the Defense and Security of the same.

Unfortunately, none of the colonies' efforts were wholly successful. England controlled the colonies' laws, and some of the most powerful men in England had money invested in the slave trade. They were determined to let nothing hinder it. So, in one way or another, most of the new laws were vetoed or ignored. Both slavery and the slave trade went on growing. Even Georgia soon was importing slaves, in spite of her founders' good intentions.

Times were changing, nevertheless. Presently the colonists came to resent being governed by England, with so little control over their own affairs.

At first they merely objected to some of the worst of England's laws, and to paying taxes which they thought unfair. When it became clear that the English government would pay no attention to their protests, they began to grow angry. Leaders in many of the colonies began to speak out more boldly, defying all English rule. Then British troops sent by King George III landed in several colonial cities, and that only made matters worse.

Before long a spirit of actual revolution—a fierce desire for liberty and complete independence—rolled through every colony like a rising ocean tide. Few white men thought of all this in connection with their black slaves. But the slaves had eyes and ears; they could see and hear what was going on.

They too began to feel that rising tide of liberty.

6. The War for Liberty

One raw and snowy March evening in 1770, a squad of British soldiers marched briskly down King Street in Boston, Massachusetts. They had orders to drive away a crowd of angry people who had gathered there.

Taunts and jeers filled the air as the soldiers advanced. The crowd began to pelt them with stones and snowballs. A British officer snapped out a command. The redcoats—so-called because of the bright red jackets of their uniforms—wheeled into line and aimed their muskets. Still the crowd pressed forward, shouting and throwing stones. Suddenly the redcoats fired.

Eleven men tumbled to the ground. Three were dead, two others mortally wounded. The rest of the people slowly fell back and finally went away, but they were angrier than ever.

This incident became famous in American history as

the Boston Massacre. It was one of the first clashes which eventually led the colonies to go to war with England for their independence—and the first man who fell on that March evening was black. We know very little about him except his name: Crispus Attucks. He was a sailor and probably a free man, though he may have been a runaway slave.

The people of Boston honored Crispus Attucks as a hero. For three days his body lay in state in a large public hall, and hundreds mourned at his funeral. He was the first man to die in the cause of American liberty, but he would not be the last.

Five years later, on April 19, 1775, the War of Independence began.

A troop of British redcoats marched out of Boston to seize a store of guns and ammunition which colonial patriots had hidden in the nearby village of Concord. When the soldiers reached Lexington, they were met by a force of citizens who called themselves *minutemen* because they had agreed to band together and fight at a minute's notice. In bitter fighting that day, both at Lexington and at Concord, the British were beaten and driven back to Boston.

Black men fought at Lexington and Concord too. Among them was Lemuel Haynes, a well-known preacher in the area. Another black man by the name of Prince Estabrook was wounded there.

An engraving of the Boston Massacre by Paul Revere. Crispus Attucks is listed below the engraving as one of the "unhappy sufferers" who were killed.

One of the black soldiers who fought at Breed's Hill is seen in the thick of battle in this old print.

Within two months another battle was fought, this time at Breed's Hill just outside of Boston. The British won, though they suffered such terrible losses that their victory was a hollow one. To the very end, American volunteers stood their ground and beat off attacks by the disciplined and well-armed British. They were defeated at last only because they ran out of gunpowder for their muskets. Tales of the Americans' heroism at the Battle of Bunker Hill, as it came to be known, helped inspire the people of all the colonies to rise up and join the war against England.

Again, some of those Americans were black.

One, Peter Salem, is said to have killed the British major who had led the redcoats at Lexington and Concord. Another, Salem Poore, showed such coolness and courage under fire that several white men wrote a letter about him to the Massachusetts Legislature. He behaved, they said, "like an experienced officer as well as an excellent soldier."

Up to this point the British had been opposed only by militia forces from New England. The militia were not regular soldiers at all, but simply men who joined together to fight whenever danger threatened. Some had served only in limited campaigns against hostile Indians in the past. Some others had fought in an earlier war in which England had won North America from France. Most of the black men at Lexington, Concord, and Bunker Hill probably were free, and many had earned that freedom by serving in the militia.

As the revolution spread throughout the colonies, however, it became clear that the poorly trained militia forces could not hope to defeat the British troops by themselves. Leaders agreed that a regular army should be raised. It was called the Continental Line. But the recruiting of men for the Line at once brought up questions about black soldiers. Some white men feared they could not be trusted. Naturally enough, such fears were strongest among slave owners in the South. Other white men pointed out that allowing slaves to take part in a war for freedom was sure to give them ideas which could lead to nothing but trouble in the end.

Not everyone shared these views, by any means. Many farsighted leaders argued that black men as well as white were entitled to fight for their liberty. James Otis, a member of the new Continental Congress from Massachusetts, declared flatly that all slaves ought to be set free at once. Alexander Hamilton of New York and James Madison of Virginia, among others, urged that every slave be given the opportunity to win his freedom as a soldier.

It was obvious to everyone, however, that the colonies never would win their war against England if they started to fight among themselves. When the slave owners still refused to approve of black soldiers, therefore, they finally had their way. Soon after General George Washington took command of the Continental Line in June, 1775, he issued an order barring black men from the army. Later the order was changed so that black men who already were serving could remain. But no others, either slave or free, would be permitted to enlist.

The war for liberty had barely begun—and already the black man was denied a part in it.

The British—supposedly the enemies of liberty—never adopted this shortsighted policy. From the first there had been men in every colony who opposed a revolution against England. They were known as Tories. When open fighting broke out, these Tories had a hard decision to make. Many of them chose to remain loyal to the mother country rather than to join their fellow colonists. In order to encourage such loyalty and to punish the rebels, several British officials in America issued proclamations which promised freedom to all slaves belonging to rebellious colonists if they would leave their masters and go over to the British side.

It was a telling blow, for it hit the slave owners right where they could be hurt most. A Virginia man said later that two of his neighbors "lost every slave they had in the world . . . This has been the general case of all those who were near the enemy." The owner of a large plantation in South Carolina lamented that *he* lost "eighty-eight prime Negroes and eight inferior ones."

All in all, many thousands of slaves seized their chance for freedom by running away to join the British.

Very few of them became soldiers. The English army needed strong labor detachments, as all armies do, and it was here that the runaway slaves rendered valuable service indeed. They helped to dig earthworks and build forts. They drove supply wagons, shod horses, repaired bridges and roads. Some of the bravest black men volunteered to act as spies. Still pretending to be slaves, they were able to pass through the American lines without attracting much attention or arousing suspicion. Often they brought back valuable information.

The British Navy made good use of runaways who were sailors. Some of these knew the crooked, reef-strewn channels off the American coasts well enough to become pilots aboard British men-of-war. A black man, known only as Sampson, proved to be such a fine pilot that his captain took special care to protect him. On one occasion, when the ship was fired on by an American fort on the Carolina coast, Sampson was ordered to a safe place below decks.

On the American side, too, black men soon got their chance to serve. General Washington's ban on black soldiers failed to last very long.

British armies began to win victory after victory as their superiority in numbers and equipment took effect. The American government was short of money to buy supplies. Soldiers in the Continental Line were poorly clothed and ill-fed. Often they received no pay for months at a time. Some grew so discouraged that they deserted and went home. Other men refused to join the army because they saw only scant hopes of winning.

Presently recruiting officers took to signing up any

man they could get, regardless of the color of his skin. Black men who enlisted were promised the same pay as whites. They were promised bounties of free government land, just as white soldiers were. When state legislatures were asked to raise new regiments, they too accepted black men. Some slave owners sent their slaves into the army as a means of staying out themselves. Others brought their slaves along when they enlisted. Virginia passed a law granting freedom to all such slaves who served faithfully for a three-year period. Similar laws already were in effect in the northern colonies.

Both Georgia and South Carolina, however, still fearful of slave revolts, refused to let black men be soldiers. The white people there held out to the very end, though it cost them dearly. Some of the worst American defeats were suffered in the Deep South.

Everywhere else black men served side by side with whites. We know few of their names today, for the muster rolls frequently listed them only as "A Negro," or "A Negro Man." They made good soldiers, all the same. One Rhode Island regiment was made up almost entirely of black men. During the Battle of Rhode Island in 1778, this regiment proved that black soldiers were the equals of any white men.

An American force which included the black regiment had set out to capture the town of Newport. Scarcely had the battle begun than the Americans found themselves so badly outnumbered that they were forced to retreat. Seeing the chance for a great victory, the enemy pursued them hard. British officers had found out that the Rhode Island regiment was a new one, inexperienced and poorly trained as yet. It should be easy to break through the black men's line, they thought, and then the whole American force might be destroyed.

A crack British regiment of mercenaries—tough professional soldiers called Hessians—charged the Rhode Island position. The black men stood firm. A well-aimed volley from their muskets sent the redcoats stumbling back in disorder. Quickly they formed ranks and charged again, bayonets gleaming as they came on through drifting clouds of powder smoke. Again the black soldiers beat them off. The Hessians charged a third time, and once more the black line stopped them in their tracks. That ended it. The Hessians were brave men, but they were too badly battered to fight on.

In his report of the battle General John Sullivan, the American commander, made a point of mentioning the black soldiers' "desperate valor." He gave them much of the credit for preventing a serious defeat.

Colonel Christopher Greene, the white officer in charge of this Rhode Island regiment, was killed some years later in another fight at Points Bridge, New York. A detachment of his black soldiers died with him in a heroic effort to save his life.

Throughout the war other black men gave good accounts of themselves in many of the bitterest campaigns. There was even a black woman, Deborah Gannett by name, who distinguished herself as a soldier. Disguised as a man, she served in a Massachusetts regiment for more than a year before she was finally found out and sent back home. In signing her discharge papers, her commanding officer wrote that she had been "a faithful and gallant soldier, and at the same time preserving the virtue and chastity of her sex . . . and is discharged from the service with a fair and honorable character."

On the sea as well, black men did not always do their fighting under the British flag. The American Continental Navy was small, with only a few warships, but it needed men quite as badly as did the land forces. Records show that the ships' crews often included black sailors.

Like the British, many American captains were glad to have them for pilots. This was especially true in southern waters, where many of the sailor-slaves had been pilots during peacetime. A Virginia slave named Caesar earned high praise for the skill and courage he showed in helping the schooner *Patriot* capture a ship loaded with supplies for the British army. James Forten, another black sailor, went to sea as a powder boy when he was only fourteen years old. His ship was captured by a British man-of-war, and he spent several months as a prisoner, though he could have gone free at any time had he been willing to join the enemy. Many years later Forten became a sailmaker with a prosperous business of his own.

By 1783, when England gave up at last and granted independence to the colonies, thousands of slaves had won their freedom on one side or the other. Slave owners, however, were bitterly angry about those who had run away and joined the British. For a long time they argued that the peace treaty should compel England to return all the runaways to their American masters. But English leaders refused to do so. They had made a bargain, and they kept it. When the British troops sailed away, the black men went with them, to be settled as free men in other British colonies.

Some found new lives and new homes in Nova Scotia, Canada. Others were taken to England. Still others—about 400 of them—eventually landed in Sierra Leone, West Africa, as the first settlers in a new British colony to be made up entirely of slaves who had been set free.

The freed slaves on the American side found themselves in a brand-new nation, and only the future could tell what was to come of that.

7. The Rights of Man

From the very beginning, many thoughtful leaders of the American Revolution were troubled by the black man's status. They had gone to war in the name of freedom and the rights of man. If they were sincere believers in those rights, they could not honestly deny them to black people any more than to white.

Yet that was precisely what slavery did.

Many of the most outstanding leaders themselves owned slaves. General George Washington, for example, was a Virginia plantation owner with a large force of slave workers. Commodore Esek Hopkins, the first commander of the Continental Navy, was a former slaver captain who had once quelled a bloody slave mutiny aboard his ship. There were a host of others who were by no means ready to do away with slavery, or even to admit that it was wrong.

As early as 1776, when the Continental Congress asked Thomas Jefferson to write the colonies' Declaration of Independence, the problem had begun to cause serious arguments. Today everyone remembers these stirring words from the Declaration:

> We hold these truths to be self-evident, that all men are created equal, that they are endowed by their Creator with certain unalienable rights, that among these are Life, Liberty and the pursuit of Happiness . . .

It is not so well known, however, that Jefferson then went on to list the colonists' various grievances against King George III of England. One of them was:

> He has waged civil war against human nature itself, violating its most sacred rights of life and liberty, in the persons of a distant people who never offended him; captivating them and carrying them into slavery . . . or to incur miserable death in their transportation thither . . .

Most of the colonies had tried for a long time to enact laws which would stop or limit the slave trade. They had objected loudly when England had vetoed or ignored these laws, thus encouraging slavery. Yet the delegates to the Continental Congress from South

Carolina and Georgia would not sign the first draft of the Declaration, which blamed the king for the slave trade. They wanted nothing at all said about the buying and selling of slaves or about slavery, and the delegates from several other colonies agreed with them.

As Jefferson himself wrote sometime afterward: "Our Northern brethren also, I believe, felt a little tender under these censures; for though their people have very few slaves themselves, yet they have been pretty considerable carriers of them to others."

The paragraph had to be taken out, therefore, and the whole troublesome slavery question was avoided.

Thomas Jefferson was disappointed. Though a Virginian with a plantation and slaves of his own, he was deeply concerned over the evils of slavery. As he declared some years later: "Indeed, I tremble for my country when I reflect that God is just; that His justice cannot sleep forever." Later still, toward the end of his life, he summed up the problem in a letter to a friend. "We have the wolf by the ears," he wrote, "and can neither hold him nor safely let him go. Justice is in one scale and self-preservation in the other."

It was true. The whole system of life in the South had depended on slavery for much too long. Other men who lived there realized, as Jefferson did, that slavery was wrong. Yet no one could see any practical way of putting an end to it.

Thus, while the war for liberty was fought and won, slavery went on as before.

Nevertheless, the years following the war's end brought important gains for many black people. In some parts of the North, so many slaves had earned their freedom by serving in the army that slavery was virtually wiped out. This happened in both Vermont and New Hampshire. There were far fewer slaves left in every northern state, for the same reason. Equally encouraging was the fact that the war had left strong antislavery feelings among northern whites in general.

In 1780 Pennsylvania became the first state to take steps to abolish slavery by law. By the year 1804, or shortly afterward, all other northern states had done likewise. Most of their new laws provided that the remaining slaves were to be freed only gradually, because they might compete for jobs with poor white workers if too many were freed all at once. Some states made the process very gradual indeed. New York's law, for example, granted freedom to a female slave only after twenty-five years of service to her master. A male slave had to serve for twenty-eight years.

Taken as a whole, however, such laws spelled the end of slavery throughout the North.

In 1787 the Congress forbade slavery in the vast Northwest Territory, which included all the lands

Philadelphia in the early 1800s boasted a thriving free black community. This picture of black workmen was painted by Pavel Svinin, a Russian visitor.

lying north of the Ohio River and west to the Mississippi. To be sure, this act had very little effect at the time. Most of the region still was a wilderness inhabited only by Indian tribes which acknowledged no allegiance to any white man's government. Moreover, the law was passed only on condition that all the territory south of the Ohio should remain open to slavery. In addition, all runaway slaves who fled into the Northwest Territory had to be returned to their masters if they were caught.

Southern members of Congress insisted on these two provisions. In spite of them, nevertheless, the law meant that black men and women would be assured of freedom in the great future states of Ohio, Indiana, Illinois, Michigan, and Wisconsin.

There were other gains as time went by. Many white people realized that the former slaves would not find it easy to make their way in the world as free men. Schools to train them were set up. One of the first was the African Free School, founded by the New York Manumission Society in 1787. It opened with forty students. Soon there were similar schools in nearly every northern city.

Classes were often held for black children during the day and for black men and women at night. When these freed people had been trained, they were given help in finding jobs. School officials frequently checked afterwards to make sure that black workers were being treated fairly by their employers.

Because they were usually segregated in white churches, black men and women soon founded congregations of their own in almost all faiths. Such groups became important agencies of self-help for black people. Many outstanding leaders at that time, in fact, were black ministers. A few came to be so well known that they were asked to preach in white churches as well as black.

Various societies for the betterment of black people reached out in all directions. They went on urging state legislatures to pass more laws benefitting the black man, slave as well as free. They did their best to make sure that masters and employers obeyed the laws already in force. They worked tirelessly against everything connected with slavery and the slave trade. In fact, these societies were the founders of the *Abolitionist* movement, which was destined to grow and become stronger in the years ahead.

The task they had set for themselves was difficult and often discouraging. The vast majority of white people everywhere still thought of black people as members of a lower race who simply did not have the ability to be the white man's equal. This view was common even among the Abolitionists themselves. Their efforts to help black men were due to kindness

Benjamin Banneker   Phillis Wheatley

rather than to any true belief in black equality. Yet some black men and women succeeded in becoming shining examples to their own people and to whites alike.

Two of the most noted during this period were Phillis Wheatley and Benjamin Banneker.

Phillis Wheatley had been born in Africa. She was still a small child when slave traders captured her, carried her across the sea, and sold her in Boston. Fortunately, she fell into the hands of a good master who saw that she received an education equal to that of most white children of the time. The little girl quickly learned Latin and became acquainted with classical English literature. Taken to church with her master's own family, she became deeply religious. Soon her intelligence and charm made her a favorite of the entire white congregation.

Phillis began to write poetry when she was still a girl in her teens. Gradually her poetry began to attract widespread attention in the Boston area. Later she visited England, and there, too, people were charmed and amazed by her talent. Many years after her death a collection of her poetry, published by Abolitionist societies and titled *The Memoir and Poems of Phillis Wheatley* still was being read and admired.

Benjamin Banneker's story was even more remarkable. Unlike Phillis Wheatley, he was born free, though his father had first been brought into Maryland as a slave. In school young Benjamin showed such cleverness at science and arithmetic that some of his white teachers loaned him extra books and urged him to go on studying. Eventually the boy grew up to be an astronomer and a mathematician whose work was honored by leading scientists in both this country and Europe. For several years he wrote and published one of America's first almanacs. He also learned to be an excellent surveyor.

Banneker's prominence was recognized when he was asked to serve with a national commission to plan and survey the city of Washington, new capital of the United States. Very few white men of his time, or of any time, could match his record of success in so many different fields.

There were not many like Banneker and Phillis Wheatley, of course. Few black men or women were lucky enough to be given the advantages and encouragement they received. On the contrary, the majority of freed slaves had to overcome the serious handicaps of ignorance, humility, and unthinking obedience which had been forced on them during years of bondage. All too often they found that freedom brought only hard work, disappointment, and bewildering new problems. Yet these final years of the 1700s were better than most black people ever had known in the past. Even in many parts of the South, the old black codes governing slavery no longer were strictly enforced.

On May 25, 1787 a convention met at Philadelphia, Pennsylvania to draw up a constitution for the United States. Once more the old slavery question came up for argument. Men from the South still were determined that slavery must not be ended. Even the slave trade, they insisted, must be allowed to continue. They were ready to agree that it was an evil thing, perhaps, but a necessary evil.

The War of Independence had left many plantation owners worried about their supply of slaves.

The British, as we have seen, had freed thousands of slaves and taken them out of the country. Many more had run away during the war. Most states—even Maryland and Virginia in the South—already had made the slave trade illegal. Considering these facts, said the delegates from South Carolina and Georgia, it would be unfair to stop the trade until they had had time to bring in the new slaves they needed.

At last, since neither North nor South would give in completely, a compromise was reached.

By its terms, the words *slave, slavery,* and *Negro* did not appear anywhere in the final draft of the Constitution of the United States. Thus, the issue was sidestepped once again, and slavery was neither approved nor disapproved. In return, northern delegates agreed that the federal government could do nothing to stop the slave trade for a period of at least twenty years.

This actually amounted to a pretty poor "compromise" from the northern point of view. By saying nothing, it accepted the existence of slavery; worse than that, it shamefully ignored the moral principles involved and belied the glowing words of the Declaration of Independence. In justice to the northern delegates, however, it is doubtful that *any* constitution could have been adopted without the compromise. The slavery interests simply were too powerful, too determined, and too firmly united.

Another argument arose over the number of men the states should elect to Congress. It was soon decided that they should each have two senators, while the number of members a state could send to the House of Representatives would depend on that state's population. But then the South claimed that slaves ought to be counted as well as white men. The northern delegates objected. Slaves were not permitted to vote, they pointed out. Slaves were not citizens at all. Indeed, the southern states' own laws gave them no human rights of any kind, so it made no sense to count them on the same basis as free men.

In the end another compromise was arranged. This one provided that southern states might count *three-fifths* of their slaves, but no more. Even that granted them a great deal more power in the government than they would have had otherwise. Yet many northern delegates felt that it scarcely mattered, because slavery already was dying out. As one of them, Oliver Ellsworth of Connecticut, put it:

"Slavery in time will not be a speck in our country!"

Mr. Ellsworth undoubtedly meant well, and his opinion probably was shared by a good many others. But he was a very bad prophet. Slavery was not dying. Within a few years it began to grow stronger and more widespread than ever.

8. The Cotton Kingdom

When the Constitution of the United States was drafted, mighty forces already were at work in both Europe and America. Hardly anyone realized it at the time, but those forces were about to bring far-reaching changes in the lives of everyone, white and black alike.

They had begun with the invention of the steam engine by a Scotsman named James Watt in the year 1769. Watt's first engine was a crude affair, but soon improved models of it were being used to run all sorts of new machines. The machines, in turn, were able to do a wide variety of jobs that always had been done by men or by beasts of burden in the past. The machines did the work faster and more cheaply than ever before. Slowly at first, but steadily too, goods began to be turned out by large factories instead of by craftsmen working in their own homes or small shops.

This movement, known as the *Industrial Revolution,* eventually created the world in which we live today. Among the earliest changes it brought to America was a new and valuable crop for the South—cotton.

Planters had begun to grow a little cotton in the

This early cotton gin made it possible for a few slaves to separate large quantities of cotton lint from seeds, thus making cotton a profitable crop for their owner.

colonies long before the War of Independence. Most of it was made into cloth by means of small spinning wheels and looms which were worked by hand. The work was usually done by the women of individual families, who used the cloth for their own needs. Raising cotton for sale did not become profitable until machines were developed in England to spin it into thread and then to weave the thread into cloth on a larger scale. Even then the crop had one great drawback which held the profits down.

The soft cotton fibers in the pods, or bolls, clung to the seeds so tightly that picking them apart was a long and tedious task. The most skillful slave, working as hard as possible, could separate only about a pound of lint, as it was called, in a whole day's time. Thus it was next to impossible to prepare large quantities for market. The problem was only partly solved by the introduction of sea island cotton, a new variety in which the lint was somewhat easier to separate.

Then Eli Whitney, a young schoolteacher from New England, built the first mechanical cotton gin while visiting a Georgia plantation in 1793. His machine consisted of rollers studded with metal teeth which pulled the cotton lint through a wire screen but left the seeds behind. It worked so simply that a single slave, doing little more than turning a crank, was able to produce as much as fifty pounds of lint a day.

Plantation owners were quick to see the advantages of Whitney's machine. Presently bigger and better gins, driven by steam engines, were built. These could turn out still more lint. Soon cotton production began to rise like magic.

Almost overnight—inside of a very few years, actually—cotton became the most important crop in the South.

Records still in existence show some of the enormous profits that were made. A South Carolina planter grew rich enough to retire in the three years from 1796 to 1798. He sold his plantation at a price most of his neighbors felt was far too high. Yet the man who bought it made every cent of the price back from the cotton he raised in the next two years. Another man, who planted cotton on 300 acres, figured out the value of the crop according to the number of slaves who worked on it. Each slave, he discovered, had earned $509 for him. Considering that such a plantation might employ a hundred slaves or more—often many times that number—the prospect of making large sums of money was excellent indeed.

Figures like these were not unusual, and they spoke for themselves. As it happened, cotton came along just when many plantation owners were beginning to complain of hard times. The profits from raising tobacco had been falling steadily for years. Some slave owners were feeling the pinch so badly that there was a rueful little joke among them. Instead of runaway slaves, they said, the country would soon be hearing of runaway masters.

Now all that was changed. Large gangs of slaves became more valuable than ever to their masters.

Cotton was well suited to the use of slave labor. In the mild southern climate it grew all year 'round, so there were few slack seasons during which slaves failed to earn their keep. The plow and the hoe were the only tools needed for cultivation. Picking the cotton under the hot sun was a tiresome form of drudgery, but it required no great physical strength. Old as well as young, women and even little children, could be put to work at it. Besides, cotton was a hardy crop. Not even careless handling could damage the bolls very badly. It was much more satisfactory in this respect than tobacco, which required both care and skill.

Unlike rice, which could be raised only in the warm, wet lowlands along the seacoast, cotton grew well in almost all kinds of southern soil. Best of all, from the plantation owners' point of view, the operators of textile mills in England—and later in the northern states too—were greedy for all the raw cotton they could get. No matter how much was raised, prices and profits remained high.

Wealth began to increase rapidly throughout the

South. Planters built large, splendid homes for themselves and their families. Their wives and daughters enjoyed costly gowns and bonnets from Paris. Their sons went to expensive schools or took long pleasure trips to Europe. In effect, these people became the rulers of a new American kingdom: the cotton kingdom, based on cheap slave labor.

Cotton was one of the factors which encouraged southern pioneer families to move into frontier regions to the west. Most of these people were small farmers. Few of them owned slaves, and many never would. But among them were ambitious men who realized that cotton offered their best hope for success and prosperity in the future. They looked forward to settling on new, virgin land and becoming planters and slave owners as soon as possible.

Tennessee was admitted to the Union as a state in 1796. By that time, some men there already had begun to raise small amounts of cotton. They shipped it to market in a long and roundabout way, on flatboats which floated down the Cumberland and Mississippi Rivers to New Orleans. Farther to the south and west, other frontier territories also were attracting settlers. There, too, the soil and climate proved ideal for growing cotton. The time was not far distant when those territories would become Mississippi and Alabama, two of the greatest cotton states of all.

The cotton kingdom was growing, and as it grew, its power in Congress steadily increased.

All this meant new life for the slave trade. Cargoes of black men and women fresh from Africa were eagerly sought after by buyers in the seaports of Georgia and South Carolina. In addition, a slave trade grew up among the states themselves, despite the fact that most of them had laws forbidding it. Tobacco planters in Virginia and Maryland, finding themselves with more slaves than they could support, were only too happy to sell some of them to the cotton planters in other states.

As slave owners began to sell their "surplus" slaves to others, sad processions of black men and women became a common sight in southern cities.

With money to be made, the laws were soon repealed, changed, or simply not enforced.

Increasing prosperity brought a new attitude toward slavery itself. Southerners no longer were willing to admit that it was a "necessary evil," as many of them once had. Instead, they took to calling it a positive force for good. Several years later, when this feeling had become general in every southern state, a Virginia attorney named George Fitzhugh wrote a book defending it. Said he:

> The negro slaves of the south are the happiest, and, in some sense, the freest people in the world. The children and the aged and infirm work not at all, and yet have all the comforts and necessities of life provided for them. They enjoy liberty, because they are oppressed neither by care nor labor.

Perhaps some people honestly believed this nonsense. A great many others undoubtedly knew better but preferred to convince themselves that it was true. For every farseeing man like Thomas Jefferson and a few like him, there were hundreds more who refused to be concerned about slavery at all.

Similar points of view became general even in

the North. Abolitionist societies, alarmed and horrified by the spread of slavery, continued their efforts to fight it. But a kind of hostile reaction had set in among other white people. The enthusiasm for liberty and the rights of man which had swept the country for a while was dying down. Much of it always had been more words than action, to be sure; now, even the words were forgotten. Many white people felt that black men already had received enough help and ought to shift for themselves. Resentment was growing among poor and unskilled white workers who claimed free black men were taking their jobs away.

Much of this was natural, no doubt. Nevertheless, it meant a severe setback for the black man's long, hard march toward true freedom and equality. For the thousands of slaves in southern cotton fields, freedom had become a lost hope. This was the state of affairs when a new black hero arose to kindle that hope anew.

Word of him came across the sea from the West Indies, where slavery in America had first begun.

9. Toussaint L'Ouverture

Ideas about liberty and equality for all men were not confined to the United States alone. Over much of Europe toward the close of the eighteenth century, a new spirit of freedom based on the rights of man was taking hold. In England and several other countries this feeling led to a growing disgust with the slave trade and a general movement to put an end to it. In France it went still further.

There, the people rose up and overthrew their king in a long and bloody revolution which began in 1789. Soon the revolution spread to France's colony on the West Indian island of San Domingo. That brought it uncomfortably close to the United States—and to southern slave owners.

Conditions in San Domingo were similar in many ways to those in our southern states. Sugar had been the island's main crop for many years. Just as cotton was soon to do in the American South, sugar had brought wealth and luxury to a ruling class of white masters who used slave labor to work their vast plantations. But

San Domingo also had a large population of free mulattoes. They were much more numerous there than in the American South, and their status among the French was a peculiar one.

Many were wealthy and well educated. Some had large plantations and black slaves of their own and were even accepted socially, to some extent, by the ruling whites. At the same time, however, they were denied most of the rights and privileges of white men. Because of this—and inspired by the revolution going on in France, the mother country—the mulattoes were the first to revolt against the San Domingan government.

The revolt failed. Its leaders were captured and brutally put to death. But the island's troubles had only begun, for almost at once the slaves rose up in rebellion too.

What provided the spark that led them to do so is uncertain, though no doubt news of the French Revolution had reached them also. Perhaps they hoped to win their freedom by joining the mulattoes. If so they were badly mistaken, for the mulattoes were quite as opposed to freeing the slaves as the white masters were.

Whatever caused them to act, the black men and women of the island were angry people, filled with fury by long years of cruelty and hardship. In a series of merciless attacks they killed more than 2,000 white men, women, and children. Hundreds of plantation houses were burned. Fields and crops were destroyed. When French troops marched against them, the rebellious slaves retreated to the forests and mountains of the island's interior and went on fighting from there. Within a few months vast areas of San Domingo lay in ruins.

Little was done to improve matters. White officials were torn by quarrels among themselves. Mulattoes and whites still hated and mistrusted one another. The revolutionary government in faraway France was weak and uncertain of its own leadership. Many white men gave up and fled from the island in despair. One of them described how hopeless the situation appeared to him:

> One of three things will follow: the whites will exterminate the whole mulatto caste; the mulattoes will destroy the whites; or the negroes will profit by these dissensions to annihilate both the whites and the mulattoes. But in any case, San Domingo will be erased from the maps of Europe.

Finally the French government tried to bring peace by promising freedom and full rights as French citizens to black men and mulattoes as well as to whites.

Even that failed. In spite of all that had happened, many white masters still refused to agree to free their slaves. Knowing that, the slaves were afraid to believe the government's promise. At this point, too, the rebel black men had broken up into many different bands. Each band had its own leaders, and some of these leaders had begun to fight each other.

A strong man was needed—a true black leader who could speak for all his people—and at last such a man appeared. His name was Pierre Dominique Toussaint L'Ouverture.

Though he claimed to be descended from an African king, Toussaint L'Ouverture had been born a slave in San Domingo. No doubt he received more advantages than most, for his master selected him to serve as his coachman, an unusually privileged position for a slave. Little is known of his early life, however, up to the time he joined one of the rebel slave bands. Soon he rose to become its commander. He proved to be a brave and clever leader, and his reputation grew. In time, other rebel parties united under his leadership.

Now he showed that he was not only a fighter, but a wise statesman as well.

Toussaint's first move was to accept the French offer of liberty and citizenship for his people. In return for his pledge of loyalty to France, he was made a general in the French army. By promising fair and just

Toussaint L'Ouverture

peace terms to rival black leaders, he won most of them over to his side. Next came the problem of restoring order and prosperity to San Domingo. It was not easy. Nearly all business activity had come to a stop. The widespread fighting and destruction had left the unfortunate people of the island on the verge of starvation.

Toussaint met this emergency by permitting some of the white and mulatto masters to return to their plantations. He induced black men and women to go back to work in the fields by setting up a new system which gave them a share of all the crops they raised. This made them more than free workers; it gave them part-ownership too. The system worked. Gradually the island's commerce began to revive.

Yet so many new difficulties arose that a lesser man than Toussaint would have been discouraged. A war had broken out between France and England. Presently a strong British fleet appeared off the coast of San Domingo. An army came ashore, prepared to seize the island for England. Many of the wealthy mulattoes, and even some of the remaining French plantation owners, immediately joined the invaders. Bitterly resentful of being governed by a black man, they hoped that the British would restore slavery as it had been before.

Undaunted, Toussaint raised a powerful black army and fought the new enemy to a standstill.

He was helped by an epidemic of yellow fever among the British soldiers. Because San Domingans had often been exposed to yellow fever, they were less likely to catch the disease. The Englishmen, however, fell ill and died by the hundreds. Finally, those who were left boarded their ships and sailed away again. But not even this victory ended Toussaint's troubles.

A mulatto leader named André Rigaud still held out against him from a stronghold in the southern part of the island. In order to overcome this new threat, Toussaint was forced to make secret agreements with both England and the United States. In return for their help, he promised to let them share the control of all San Domingo's foreign trade. He also confided to them that his real goal was complete independence for San Domingo, in spite of his oath of loyalty to France.

Since the British were enemies of France, they were quite willing to supply Toussaint with some badly needed war materials. In the United States the merchants of New England considered their trade with San Domingo so valuable that they persuaded the government to become Toussaint's ally too, though southern slave owners objected violently.

What Toussaint actually was doing, of course, was bargaining for help of any kind, wherever he could get it. And again he was successful. Warships sent from the United States bombarded and destroyed André Rigaud's fortress. Rigaud himself was forced to flee from the island and seek refuge in France. Toussaint was the undisputed ruler of San Domingo at last.

He drew up a constitution which made him the head of the government for the rest of his life. Then he felt secure enough to take his last and greatest step; he proclaimed that French rule was at an end forever.

That was Toussaint's first serious mistake, for a powerful general named Napoleon Bonaparte had made himself the supreme authority in France. Bonaparte, in fact, already had conquered most of Europe and was now planning to build a vast American empire for France. He saw at once that Toussaint would have to be removed, for a free San Domingo would make his plan impossible. He promptly sent an army to take possession of the island. The leaders of that army had secret orders to force black San Domingans back into slavery if necessary.

Somehow, word of the secret orders leaked out. It aroused the fighting spirit of Toussaint's followers as nothing else could have done, and they rallied around him to defend their hard-won liberty.

Scarcely had the French troops landed when there was another outbreak of yellow fever. For a while it appeared that the epidemic was about to win another victory for Toussaint, just as the previous one had saved San Domingo from the British. Then, however, the great black leader was beaten by treachery. General Leclerc, the French commander, invited him to a meeting under a flag of truce in order to discuss peace terms. When Toussaint accepted in good faith, Leclerc's soldiers seized him and carried him aboard a waiting French man-of-war.

The ship immediately set sail for France, where Toussaint was thrown into prison. He never regained his freedom. Badly treated by his jailers and worn out by years of struggle, he died in prison in April, 1803.

Toussaint L'Ouverture had ruled San Domingo for only a short time. His rule had been a stormy one, filled with constant battles against one enemy after another. Through it all, nevertheless, his fame had spread far beyond the island, making him a hero to black people everywhere. The shameful betrayal by France had made him a martyr as well. But his dream of independence for his country was not in vain.

Another former slave, Jean Jacques Dessalines, took Toussaint's place and carried on the war with France. Yellow fever still raged among the French soldiers. General Leclerc himself died of it. Before a year had passed, the survivors of his weakened army left the island, and Dessalines was victorious.

He was a much grimmer, harder man than Toussaint L'Ouverture. Ruthlessly he killed or drove away the last remaining white people, making San Domingo a wholly black country. He issued orders forbidding all the old distinctions between black men and mulattoes, and he saw to it that the orders were enforced without mercy. In 1804 Dessalines changed the island's name to Haiti and had himself crowned emperor. The Frenchman's prediction that San Domingo would be erased from the maps of Europe had come true.

What was more, for the first time anywhere in the western world, black men had succeeded in fighting their way up from slavery and founding a new nation of their own.

Every white government in Europe and America refused to recognize Haiti for many years. By its very existence, though, it caused far-reaching effects. One of them was an immediate and unexpected gain for the United States.

The loss of San Domingo was a heavy blow for Napoleon Bonaparte. Discouraged by it and beset by costly new wars in Europe, he gave up all his ambitions for an American empire. Louisiana, his other great colony in America, thus seemed of little use to him. Toward the end of 1803, only eight months after Toussaint L'Ouverture's death in prison, Bonaparte sold all of Louisiana to the United States.

It proved to be one of the greatest bargains in American history. At one stroke, for a price of some $15,000,000, this nation gained possession of the thriving commercial port of New Orleans at the mouth of the Mississippi River. Most of the broad, unexplored lands stretching north and west to the Pacific Ocean became United States territory also. With the way opened for Americans to push out into this vast new frontier, the nation's potential for growth and power was virtually unlimited.

The seeds of new problems were planted too. One day the question of freedom or slavery in the new territory would have to be settled, and that would prove troublesome. But in 1803 few Americans were looking so far ahead.

The events in San Domingo, or Haiti, already had given many of them a great deal to think about.

10. The Troubled Years

Long before Haiti became a free nation, white families fleeing from the slave rebellions there had begun to arrive in the United States. As early as 1793, the same year in which Eli Whitney built his first cotton gin, thousands of them poured into our seacoast cities.

Most of the refugees were far from penniless. Many of the first ones to leave San Domingo had had time to convert some of their wealth into cash, and to save jewelry and other valuable possessions. Many, too, were able to bring some of their slaves with them. The majority of these people settled in various places in the South where the warm climate and the white society based on plantation life were much like those they had known at home. Thus they lived quite comfortably.

Their presence, however—and the presence of their slaves—soon led to confusion and unrest. The refugees, of course, had frightening tales to tell of the bloodshed, suffering, and destruction caused by the slave uprisings. American slave owners listened with sympathy at first, and then with growing dread and indignation. Remembering past slave plots or rumors of plots in their own neighborhoods, they could imagine no worse calamity than a revolution of black men and women in America. All at once, the possibility of such a revolution began to seem very real indeed.

American slaves also quickly learned of the San Domingo rebellion. Some probably overheard their masters talking about it. Others mingled with the Frenchmen's slaves and listened eagerly to their stories of what had happened. Undoubtedly some masters tried to prevent this, but it was impossible. As one worried white man explained: "Negroes have a wonderful art of communicating intelligence; it will run several hundred miles in a week or a fortnight."

Before long, word of Toussaint L'Ouverture's great deeds reached even the humblest slaves all over the South. His success filled them with pride and with a renewed sense of black men's rightful destiny as human beings. A great deal of the resulting unrest was vague and without any plan, but it spread rapidly.

In that same year of 1793 an official of Portsmouth, Virginia wrote to the state's governor asking for help in quelling the disturbances which were becoming common in the vicinity. He described one incident:

> Our town swarms with strange negroes, foreign and domestic, who have already begun hostilities upon themselves. Last night at half past eleven, four were found hanging twenty steps from my door, upon a cedar tree... We have many hundreds of French negroes landed in this town. It was four of them that were hanged as above. They are divided. The Household family negroes are trusty and well disposed, but many others did belong to the insurrections...

Apparently no one ever found out why the four French slaves were hanged, or who did it. The most obvious and frightening suspicion, though, was that they might have been the victims of fellow slaves who blamed them for refusing to join in a revolt.

Similar disorders occurred in widely scattered parts of the South about this time. In another Virginia community, five slaves were tried and executed for attacking a white man with clubs. A New York newspaper printed a story saying that the militia had been called out and placed on guard duty in Charleston, South

Carolina, because "the Negroes have become very insolent." The paper went on to tell of an attempt to break into an army storehouse containing guns and ammunition, and then added: "It is said that the San Domingo Negroes have sown those seeds of revolt . . ."

From New Orleans, which was not yet an American possession, came news of still more slave unrest. In 1795 a plot for an uprising was discovered on a large plantation near the city. When the ringleaders were arrested and locked in jail, a group of other slaves stormed the jail in a bold effort to set them free. Soldiers drove the attackers off at last, but only after bitter fighting.

Again, the trouble was blamed on the "melancholy affair" in San Domingo.

Such events were all the more disturbing to white people because slave revolts had been almost unheard of for several years following the War of Independence. No doubt made hopeful by all the talk about liberty and the rights of man, most slaves had seemed content to bide their time for a while. Their masters, sensing this, had eased many of the harsher rules of the slave codes. It had been a time of comparative goodwill on both sides.

Now that time was over.

The slave codes were tightened and made more strict than ever. In many areas of the South, bands of white men were organized into patrols. Armed with guns and mounted on horseback, they rode about the countryside on the watch for runaways or for any slaves whose actions seemed at all suspicious. Curfews forbidding slaves to leave their quarters after nine or ten o'clock at night were rigidly enforced. All the old laws against slaves meeting together, or owning firearms, or having other privileges, came back into force with greater harshness than before. What this actually amounted to was a new form of bondage for black men and women, much worse than the slavery many of them were accustomed to.

Even slaves who had no intention of rebelling came to resent the new conditions. Some could not help showing it. Then wary masters, already half-expecting trouble, reacted by treating them still more severely.

Matters were not helped by the political situation in the United States at this time. The Federalist Party, which held power until 1800, stood for a strong central government very much like that of England. On the other side were the Republicans—actually the forerunners of our present-day Democratic Party—who were in favor of rule by the various states themselves. They also believed in as much liberty as possible for individual citizens. Thomas Jefferson was the Republicans' most important leader, and his views against slavery were well known.

It was not surprising, therefore, that many Federalist newspapers presently began to accuse the Republican Party of encouraging a spirit of revolution among the slaves. Then, as now, some people took their politics very seriously. Federalist and Republican slave owners often had hot arguments with one another, and no doubt many of the arguments were overheard by their household slaves. The slaves, in turn, spread the word among other slaves.

Thus a combination of several things—the new and harsher slave codes, the example of Toussaint L'Ouverture, and the doctrines of Thomas Jefferson— did in fact lead some courageous and spirited slaves to dream of rising up as leaders of their people.

One of them was a young man named Gabriel.

Very little is known about Gabriel today. He was a slave belonging to Thomas Prosser, a plantation owner near Richmond, Virginia. Many accounts of the time say that Prosser was an unusually cruel master. They also describe Gabriel as a giant who could neither read nor write. Apparently, though, he was familiar with the Bible. It was said, in fact, that he wore his hair long in imitation of his hero, Samson, the great Biblical strongman. A white neighbor who knew him declared that, "his courage and intellect were above his rank of life." Such a compliment seldom was paid to a slave, but in this case it obviously was deserved.

Working secretly with his brother Martin and another slave called Jack Bowler, Gabriel planned a rebellion of all the slaves in the vicinity.

It was worked out far more carefully than any slave uprising in the past. Hardly anything was overlooked. Some of the leaders were assigned the duty of collecting a secret store of weapons. Others agreed to contact the slaves on all plantations nearby. A free black man named Sam Bird was detailed to go among the Catawba Indians in the neighborhood and enlist their help. Most of these men did their jobs so well that several hundred slaves were brought into the plot within a few weeks.

On the appointed day in August 1800, Gabriel intended to lead them in a daring bid for freedom. First, the slaves planned to kill their masters. Then, a picked force of one hundred was to take possession of a bridge on the only road to Richmond. While they held the bridge, Gabriel was to lead the other slaves in a swift surprise attack on the city. Cut off from outside help, it would be captured and burned. Not all the white people there were to be slain, however.

Quakers, and some other church members who were known for their kindness to black men and women, would be spared. So would any Frenchmen in the city, probably because Gabriel had heard about the French Revolution and its doctrines of freedom and equality.

Apparently he also thought that many of the poor white people of the surrounding area might join him. If they did, he expected to make peace with the white authorities on condition that all slaves were to be set free. But even the possibility of failure had been taken into account. If things went wrong Gabriel planned to lead his people into the mountains of western Virginia. There they would build a fort and hold out to the last man.

Things did go wrong, though not in any way he had foreseen. At the last minute Gabriel was betrayed by some of his own people. Two slaves on a neighboring plantation grew frightened and told their master of the plot.

Word was sent to Governor James Monroe of Virginia, who immediately ordered out the militia and sent an armed patrol to investigate the story. Still it seemed that luck was with Gabriel. A blinding rainstorm on the day set for the rebellion caused him to postpone his plans. The men of the patrol, finding no signs of trouble, decided that the warning was a false one and relaxed their vigilance.

A plantation owner named Mosby wrote the story of what happened the very next morning:

> ... A Negro woman of my own came to me, and the first word she spoke was "you must not tell." Then she asked me

if I had heard that the negroes were going to rise. I told her I had. I then asked her when they were to meet. She said somewhere about Mr. Prosser's, and as they did not meet last night they would meet tonight. I asked how many she understood were to meet. She answered 300 or 400, some from town, some from the country, and that a number of them were to be mounted on horse-back, who were to go at a distance and kill and destroy all as they went . . .

That ended Gabriel's rebellion. Thoroughly aroused now, Mosby called the patrol together again. They swooped down on Prosser's plantation and seized twenty of the slave leaders. Though Gabriel and Jack Bowler escaped and stayed in hiding for more than a month, they too were finally captured.

At the trials which followed, only a few of the slaves confessed their parts in the plot and named others who were involved. They were spared. The rest, forty-five in all, were found guilty and put to death by hanging.

None of them deigned to beg for mercy. To the very end the judges were deeply impressed by their dignity and courage. One, whose name does not appear in the court records, spoke for all of the defendants when he said:

> I have nothing more to offer than what General Washington would have had to offer, had he been taken by the British officers and put to trial by them. I have ventured my life in endeavoring to obtain the liberty of my countrymen, and I am a willing sacrifice to their cause; and I beg, as a favor, that I may be immediately led to execution. I know that you have predetermined to shed my blood; why, then, all this mockery of a trial?

Not even a Toussaint L'Ouverture could have spoken more bravely. No white master who listened to those words in the crowded courtroom could doubt that liberty was as precious to black men as to white.

Yet, from the beginning, Gabriel's plan had had no real chance for success. The courage and dignity of black leaders alone were not enough. The odds against them were too great. Slavery was far too firmly established and too powerful to be ended unless, or until, white men themselves made up their minds to do it.

That was all too clear as the nation entered a new century, and the prospect was not encouraging.

11. Into a New Century

Eighteen hundred was a national election year in the United States. Thomas Jefferson was the Republican candidate for president, and he and other heads of the party in Virginia knew that the Federalists would try to use Gabriel's uprising to turn the voters against them. Therefore they did their best to suppress the news of it.

In the end, perhaps, it did not matter very much. Jefferson was elected president anyway. But one result of the secrecy was that little was heard about the revolt outside of Virginia. Within the state, however, it was another story. White people were thrown into panic by the affair. Rumors of other slave plots quickly spread from town to town. It is doubtful that most of them had any foundation, but the uneasiness was very real, and it lasted for many months. Even calm, sensible men who did not give in to panic were sure that they saw signs of trouble ahead.

John Randolph of Roanoke, Virginia, a prominent landowner and a respected leader throughout the South, commented during the trials of Gabriel and his fellow slaves:

> The accused have exhibited a spirit which, if it becomes general, must deluge the Southern country in blood. They manifested a sense of their rights and contempt of danger, and a thirst of revenge, which portend the most unhappy consequences.

Many who agreed with Randolph already had begun to grow unhappy about slavery. It was a time when falling prices for tobacco were causing plantation owners in Virginia and Maryland to question the value of their slave labor. Cotton, while it was already yielding immense profits in other southern states, had not yet become the South's foremost crop. For a very brief period, then, the whole future of slavery appeared to be in doubt.

Manumission was one way in which individual slave owners could settle that doubt.

John Randolph himself provided in his will that all of his slaves were to be freed after his death. So did several other Virginians, George Washington among them. But many owners were unwilling to manumit their slaves. Some had so much money invested in slaves that they felt it would be unfair to their heirs if they did so. Others pointed out that large numbers of freed slaves would only create new problems. This feeling was so common, in fact, that various plans were offered in answer to it.

Just before taking office as president, Thomas Jefferson suggested one to Governor James Monroe. He urged that Virginia buy up large tracts of western frontier land where freed slaves could be settled far from any white community. The Virginia legislature seriously considered this plan, but finally voted it down. After he became president, Jefferson suggested a similar plan for the whole United States. When Louisiana was purchased from France, it was thought for a while that free slaves might be settled there. Nothing came of it, however, because many congressmen objected that the new territory was too valuable to be given over to black settlers.

Some well-meaning people felt that Africa was the best place for America's black men and women. After all, they said, the slaves—or their ancestors— originally had come from Africa. It was their true homeland, and they ought to be happier there than anywhere else. On the surface, at least, this idea seemed to have a great deal in its favor.

One of its strongest supporters, Paul Cuffee of Massachusetts, was a free black man himself. He had gone to sea in a whaling ship as a mere boy. In time, through hard work and good business sense, he became a well-to-do merchant with several ships of his own. Cuffee first visited Sierra Leone in 1811 and evidently was impressed with the free black settlement which the British had founded there. Four years later Cuffee actually sent a group of free black men and women to West Africa in one of his ships, at his own expense. In 1817, encouraged by this first effort, a group of prominent white citizens founded the African Colonization Society to carry on Cuffee's work.

The society began with high hopes. Large sums of money were raised for ships and supplies. With the help of the United States government, land was purchased on the West African coast, and the new black colony of Liberia was established. Over a period of years, some thousands of black families were carried across the sea and settled there. The colony became an independent black republic in 1847 and remains so to this day.

Yet Liberia was no true answer to the hopes and ambitions of America's free black people.

Though their forebears had been Africans, these men and women were Americans now. Long years of slavery in the white man's country, on the white man's terms, had rooted out and crushed practically all traces of their ancient African heritage with its cultures and traditions. No matter how hard life might be for them in America, Africa seemed an unknown, alien land which offered nothing but worse hardships and unhappiness. Black people held to this point of view so persistently that the African Colonization Society gradually grew less and less active, until at last it existed in name only.

In the meantime, it was apparent to free black leaders that every plan suggested so far had one thing in common—a proposal to send free black people off to some distant place. They were regarded as a problem everywhere; nowhere did white Americans really want them.

The old feeling that black men were inferior still lingered in the northern states. Members of the white upper classes tended to shun black men and women. Among poorer white families there was dislike and even hatred for their black neighbors.

In the South, free black people were considered an actual menace. White masters believed that their example caused discontent among the slaves, leading them to want freedom also. This belief had existed since the earliest times, often with good reason, and nothing in the world could change it.

Even Thomas Jefferson, opposed to slavery though he was, agreed with those who doubted that black men and white ever could get along together. "Nature, habit, opinion, have drawn indelible lines of distinction between them," he declared. Other men, while sharing this view, were less kindly than Jefferson. Their attitude was simple and uncompromising: freedom should be made as difficult as possible for all black men.

The rapid growth of cotton profits in the Deep South, as we have seen, only added to their determination.

The laws permitting manumission had been changed steadily through the years. In many southern states it was nearly impossible for a master to free a slave, even when he wished to do so. The slave who did manage to earn his liberty by one means or another was hampered and oppressed by still more laws. Many of them were frankly intended to force him out of localities where he was not wanted. When he moved to another community—unless it was outside of the South altogether—he lived under the rule of other laws which threatened to force him back into bondage on the slightest pretext.

By the early years of the new century, no one could believe any longer that slavery was dying. It was equally clear that slave owners never would agree to do away with it under any circumstances. Still there were some gains, or apparent gains, in the fight against it.

The foreign slave trade was abolished by law in 1808. The twenty years of grace provided in the

Constitution had run out, and Congress promptly made it illegal to bring any more slaves into the country. Abolitionists were pleased, but slave owners were not greatly disturbed, for the ban did nothing to hinder slavery itself.

In some ways, indeed, outlawing the trade led to worse conditions instead of better.

Enforcement of the law proved difficult. Officials in the slave states did little to help. The United States Navy, when assigned the duty of capturing slavers on the high seas, found it had too few ships to do the job effectively. Some African slaves continued to be brought in and sold to plantation owners very much as before, though in smaller numbers. The main difference was that slaves were now smuggled into southern coastal regions by lawless men who were no better than pirates. Such men often treated their human cargoes much more cruelly than the slave traders of old.

The reduced numbers of new slaves soon led to higher prices for those already in the country. Virginia congressmen had foreseen this; it was one reason why their votes had helped to pass the new law. Virginia had many more slaves than any other state. Now it became good business for owners to send some of them into the cotton states for sale. The result was a rapid increase in the slave trade between the states.

An English traveler in Virginia about this time,

named J. S. Buckingham, has left us a vivid picture of what this meant:

> The sun was shining very hot, and in turning an angle of the road, we encountered the following group: first, a little cart drawn by one horse, in which five or six half-naked black children were tumbled like pigs together. The cart had no covering, and they seemed actually to have been *broiled* to sleep. Behind the cart marched three black women with head, neck and breasts uncovered, and without shoes or stockings; next came three men, bare-headed and half-naked, and chained together with an ox-chain. Last of all came a white man on horseback, carrying pistols in his belt . . .

Such a procession could not have looked much different from any slave coffle in far-off West Africa.

It was no wonder that slaves continued to rise up, here and there, in hopeless fights for freedom. Troops of the United States Army had to be called in to quell two serious slave revolts in Louisiana in the year 1811. A new war with England broke out in 1812. For a brief time, like the earlier War of Independence,

Black men fought valiantly with the young nation's army and navy in the War of 1812.

this too offered some slaves a chance for liberty. A few hundred bold ones did run away to join British invaders who landed on the eastern seacoast. As in that earlier war, also, other black men fought with American forces against the British on land and sea. This time, though, very few slaves won their freedom by doing so.

The return of peace brought new strength to the United States. The nation was growing, reaching westward, steadily becoming more prosperous and powerful. Slavery went on growing and thriving with it.

The black man's bondage in America now had lasted more than 200 years. They had been years of despair and promise; of fear and courage; of small, hard-won successes and bitter disappointments. Through all that, the sturdy urge toward liberty had refused to die. James McDowell, a well-known Virginian who later became the state's governor, was one who sounded the warning.

"You may place the slave where you please," he wrote. "You may put him under any process, debase and crush him as a rational being—you may do all this, and the idea that he was born to be free will survive it all."

A day was coming when that idea would be realized, but the freedom road still was a long and painful one.

Index

A

Abolitionists, 81–82, 94, 122
Africa, 7, 8, 9, 14–21, 35, 41, 82, 92, 118
  Gold Coast of, 16, 42
  Grain Coast of, 16
  Ivory Coast of, 16
  Slave Coast of, 16, 44
African Colonization Society, 119, 120
African Free School, 80
America, 12, 13, 28, 31, 44, 52, 69, 87, 95, 104, 105, 111, 120, 124.
  See also United States
American Revolution, 65–74, 75, 78, 84, 88, 109, 123
  causes of, 61–62, 63, 65
Attucks, Crispus, 65
Azurara, Gomes, 10–11

B

Balboa, Vasco Nuñéz de, 12
Banneker, Benjamin, 82 (pic), 83–84
Bird, Sam, 112
Black sailors, 65, 70, 73–74, 124
Black soldiers, 58, 63 (pic), 65, 67, 68, 69, 70, 71, 72, 73
Bonaparte, Napoleon, 102–103, 105
Boston Massacre, 63, 64 (pic), 65
Bowler, Jack, 112, 114
Breed's Hill. *See* Bunker Hill, Battle of
Bunker Hill, Battle of, 66 (pic), 67

C

Canot, Theodore, 17
Catawba Indians, 112
Charles II, King, 35
Churches, black, 60, 81
Columbus, Christopher, 12
Congress of the United States, 78, 80, 86, 92, 122
Constitution of the United States, 84, 85–86, 87, 122
Continental Congress, 68, 75, 76
Continental Line, 67, 68, 70
Continental Navy, 73, 75
Cortés, Hernando, 12
Cotton
  cultivation of, 87–88, 90 (pic), 91, 92, 117
  picking of, 88, 91
  and slavery, 89, 91, 92, 95, 121
Cotton gin, 88–89, 90 (pic), 106
Cuba, 27, 60
Cuffee, Paul, 118–119

D

de Beaumont, Gustave, 44
Declaration of Independence, 75–77, 85
Dessalines, Jean Jacques, 104

E

England, 16, 18, 31, 33, 35, 56, 57, 58, 60, 61, 62, 65, 67, 68, 69, 74, 76, 83, 88, 91, 96, 101, 110, 123
Estabrook, Prince, 65
Estevanico (Little Stephen), 12
Europe, 8, 12, 17, 28, 83, 87, 92, 96, 102, 104

F

Federalist Party, 110, 111, 116
Fitzhugh, George, 94
Florida, 56, 57, 58, 59, 60
Fort Mosa, 57–58, 60
Forten, James, 73–74
France, 16, 67, 96, 97, 98, 99, 101, 102, 103, 104, 118
Free blacks, 38, 48–49, 60, 61, 67, 68, 74, 79 (pic), 95, 119, 120
Freed slaves, 74, 78, 80, 85, 118
  churches for, 81
  education of, 81
  problems of, 84
French Revolution, 97, 112

G

Gannett, Deborah, 73
George III, King, 62, 76
Georgia, 39, 41, 61, 62, 71, 77, 85, 88, 93
Gonçalves, Antão, 7-9, 17

H

Haiti, 104, 105, 106. *See also* San Domingo
Hamilton, Alexander, 68
Haynes, Lemuel, 65
Henry, Prince of Portugal, 7, 9
Hopkins, Esek, 26-27, 75

I

Indentured black servants, 30 (pic), 31-32, 33, 34, 36, 51
Indentured white servants, 29, 31, 32, 33, 34, 35, 40, 51
Industrial Revolution, 87
Interracial marriages, 33, 40-41

J

Jefferson, Thomas, 75, 76, 77, 94, 110, 111, 116, 118, 120, 121

L

Leclerc, Charles, 103, 104
Liberia, 16, 119
Louisiana Purchase, 105, 118
L'Ouverture, Pierre Dominique Toussaint, 99-104, 100 (pic), 105, 107, 111, 115

M

Madison, James, 68
Manumission, 36, 37-38, 117-118, 121
Maryland, 39, 40, 41, 83, 85, 93, 117
Massachusetts, 16, 39, 63, 68, 73, 118
Memoir and Poems of Phillis Wheatley, The, 83

Middle Passage, 27
Mississippi, 92
Mississippi River, 80, 92, 105
Monroe, James, 113, 118
Mulattoes, 41, 97, 98, 100, 101, 104

N

New England, 28, 40, 67, 88, 102
New World, 12, 13, 28
New York, 52, 54, 68, 72, 78, 108
New York Manumission Society, 80
Niño, Pedro Alonso, 12
North Carolina, 39
Northwest Territory, 78, 80
Nova Scotia, 74

O

Otis, James, 68

P

Pennsylvania, 40, 78, 81, 84
Poore, Salem, 67
Portugal, 7, 8, 10, 12, 17
Prosser, Gabriel, 111-115, 116, 117
Prosser, Thomas, 111, 114
Punch, John, 34-35
Puritans, 39, 40

Q

Quakers, 40, 112

R

Randolph, John, 116, 117
Republican Party, 110, 111, 116
Rhode Island, 16, 26, 71, 72
Rice
  cultivation of, 41, 91
  and slavery, 41
Rigaud, André, 101, 102
Rolfe, John, 29, 31
Royal African Company, 35

S

Salem, Peter, 67
San Domingo, 96–103, 104, 105, 106, 107, 109, 111. *See also* Haiti
Sierra Leone, 16, 74, 119
Slave caravans, 14, 15 (pic), 93 (pic)
Slave codes, 84, 109–110, 111
Slave owners, 31, 32, 34, 36, 37, 38, 45, 46, 47, 48, 49, 52, 56, 69, 71, 73, 74, 75, 80, 81, 89, 91, 96, 97, 107, 109, 115, 120, 121, 122
Slave rebellions, 26–27, 50–51, 52–53, 54, 58–59, 60, 61, 97–98, 99, 106, 107, 108–109, 110, 111–115, 116, 123–124. *See also* Dessalines, Jean Jacques; Prosser, Gabriel; L'Ouverture, Toussaint
Slave sales, 29, 42, 46, 54 (pic), 93, 122
Slave ships, 18, 21, 22–23 (pic), 24, 25 (pic), 26–28
Slave trade, 9–13, 16–17, 18, 19 (pic), 20, 21, 22, 26, 28, 35, 40–41, 50, 54 (pic), 61, 62, 76, 77, 84, 92, 93 (pic), 121, 122
Slave traders, 16–18, 19, 20, 21, 26, 28, 122
Slavery
  abolishment in Pennsylvania, 78
  and the Constitution, 84–85
  laws relating to, 32–33, 34–35, 36, 37–38, 44–45, 50, 61, 76–77, 93–94, 109–110, 122
  in the North, 39–40, 44, 47, 78
  in the South, 39–40, 45, 47, 50, 77, 78, 84
  under Spanish rule, 56–58, 60
  in the West Indies, 29, 41
Slaves
  in British army, 69–70
  and Christianity, 11–12, 33, 35–36, 45
  cost of, 27–28
  education of, 45
  financial value of, 89
  and marriage, 45–46, 57
  number of, 28
  occupations of, 47–48
  rights of, 46, 57
  runaways (fugitives), 46, 55–56, 57, 58, 59, 60, 69, 70, 74, 80
  treatment of, 10–11, 14–15, 19–28, 36–37, 44–45
South Carolina, 39, 41, 56, 58, 69, 70, 71, 76–77, 85, 89, 93, 108–109
Spain, 12, 13, 16, 56, 57, 58, 60
Sugar cane, 28, 96
Sullivan, John, 72

T

Tobacco, 51, 93
  cultivation of, 33–34, 41, 89, 91
  curing of, 34, 43 (pic)
  and slavery, 41, 117
Triangle trade, 28

U

United States, 12, 84, 85, 87, 96, 101, 102, 105, 106, 110, 116, 118, 119, 124. *See also* America

V

Virginia, 29, 33, 34, 35, 36, 37, 39, 41, 47, 49, 51, 52, 55, 68, 69, 71, 73, 75, 85, 93, 94, 107, 108, 111, 113, 116, 117, 118, 122

W

War of Independence. *See* American Revolution
War of 1812, 123–124
Washington, George, 68, 70, 75, 117
West Africa, 14, 16, 28, 74, 119, 123
West Indies, 27, 28, 29, 41, 45, 52, 95
Wheatley, Phillis, 82 (pic), 83, 84
Whitney, Eli, 88, 89, 106